MOBILE
—UNDER—
SIEGE

MOBILE UNDER SIEGE

Surviving the Union Blockade

PAULA LENOR WEBB

Published by The History Press
Charleston, SC
www.historypress.net

Copyright © 2016 by Paula Lenor Webb
All rights reserved

First published 2016

Manufactured in the United States

ISBN 978.1.46711.847.7

Library of Congress Control Number: 2016938322

Notice: The information in this book is true and complete to the best of our knowledge. It is offered without guarantee on the part of the author or The History Press. The author and The History Press disclaim all liability in connection with the use of this book.

All rights reserved. No part of this book may be reproduced or transmitted in any form whatsoever without prior written permission from the publisher except in the case of brief quotations embodied in critical articles and reviews.

Contents

Foreword. A "Thousand Allurements": Mobile in 1861,
   by Lonnie A. Burnett   7
Preface   11
Acknowledgements   15

1. A Prequel: Rumors of War   17
2. August 1864: Battle of Mobile Bay   29
3. September 1864: Siege Begins   40
4. October 1864: Freedoms Sacrificed   50
5. November 1864: Denial and Survival   57
6. December 1864: The Call of Home   65
7. January 1865: Settle the Contradictions   74
8. February 1865: Speculations and Spies   83
9. March 1865: Stubbornness and Spanish Fort   92
10. April 1865: The Bitter End   101
11. After the War: Union Occupation   111

Notes   117
Bibliography   129
Index   139
About the Author   144

Foreword

A "THOUSAND ALLUREMENTS"

Mobile in 1861

One cannot fault the enthusiasm shown by many residents of, and travelers to, nineteenth-century Mobile. Local writer Thomas Cooper DeLeon's 1861 description of the port city was fairly typical:

> *Located at the head of her beautiful bay, with a wide sweep of blue water before her, the cleanly-built, unpaved streets gave Mobile a fresh, cool aspect. The houses were fine and their appointments in good, and sometimes luxurious taste. The society was a very pleasure-loving organization, enjoying the gifts of situations, of climate, and of fortune to their full.*[1]

Likewise, a popular antebellum southern periodical noted that, in Mobile, "the fine climate, the suburban attractions, and the creation of a thousand allurements, that cluster around social life, have operated much in her favor." One resident summed up the prevailing attitude by claiming that "there is no more delectable city on all the Gulf of Mexico than Mobile."[2]

Although locals could rightfully boast of Mobile, praise came from outside sources as well. William Howard Russell, a British correspondent of the *Times*, visited Mobile in 1861. Exploring Mobile's social scene, he found (probably much to the chagrin of the religious establishment) a city that "abounds in oyster saloons, drinking houses, lager beer and wine shops, and gambling and dancing places." Charmed by the cosmopolitan nature of the city, he approvingly pronounced Mobile "the most foreign looking city I have yet seen in the state."³ William Tecumseh Sherman—certainly not known for his love of southern cities—had been briefly stationed at Fort Morgan in the 1850s. In a letter to his sister, he gave his impression of the area:

> *On the river it resembles any other business city but as you leave the wharves and go back, you find beautiful streets of hotels, stores, and shops, etc., all as graciously ornamented as at New York. A little further back the streets are ornamented with trees and in front of the houses a little garden bed now and then shows a profusion of roses and shrubs—a little further and they begin to assume a beauty neatness and comfort I never elsewhere beheld.*⁴

By 1861, the city of Mobile had already compiled more than a century and a half historical record that included relocation, a period of colonial rule, deadly disease, financial struggles and several natural as well as man-made disasters. Originally settled by the French at Twenty-Seven-Mile Bluff in present-day north Mobile County, the inhabitants moved the city to its current site on the northwest shore of Mobile Bay in 1711. The outpost was governed successively by the French (1702–63), British (1763–80) and Spanish (1780–1813) before falling under United States' jurisdiction. Mobile entered the Union as part of the new state of Alabama in 1819. After the United States finally got possession of the area, the size and makeup of the city's population went through a marked change. An 1840 population of 13,621 had grown to nearly 30,000 by 1860. As the cotton kingdom expanded into what was then known as the Old Southwest, Mobile emerged as an important financial and transportation center of the cotton trade.⁵

Indeed, Mobile did have many "allurements" that appealed to the religious, charitable, educational, literary, social and entrepreneurial needs of its inhabitants. Guest or transient residents of the port could choose from several hotels—most notably the just completed Battle House. Three banks, including the Bank of Mobile, served the needs of commerce and credit. Government business could be transacted at the U.S. Customs House, while international concerns could be handled at one of thirteen foreign consulates. Nine insurance companies as well as six post office branches served the businessman and private citizen alike. Those in physical need could seek out one of three public hospitals or one of the several private institutions. Certainly the population did not suffer from a lack of social and cultural diversions. Religious denominations—Methodist, Baptist, Catholic, Episcopal, Presbyterian and African—flourished. Their meetinghouses ranged from stately cathedrals to Federal-style structures that would be "creditable to any of our larger cities" and a floating chapel anchored in Mobile Bay for the many transient seamen. Those so inclined could participate in any number of civic/social organizations, including the Masons, Odd Fellows, Franklin Society, Sons of Temperance, Temple of Honor, mystic societies, fire companies and military units. The reading public was served by four partisan daily newspapers—the *Register*, the *Advertiser*, the *Tribune* and the *Mercury*. Mobile's youth had the opportunity to attend the first public school system in the state of Alabama. A medical college trained future practitioners in surgery, anatomy, physiology, pathology, obstetrics and chemistry.[6]

These amenities notwithstanding, Mobile's primary importance came from its status as a leading cotton port and as an emerging rail center. Alabama was the second-largest cotton-producing state in the nation, and most of its bales were sold in and transported through Mobile. The port's $3,670,183 in exports was second among southern ports only to New Orleans. The Tombigbee and Alabama River systems gave Mobile a connection to the interior of the state, while Mobile Bay gave access to the Gulf of Mexico and the world markets. Additionally, Mobile was served by two railroads. The Mobile & Ohio connected the city with Columbus, Kentucky. At Corinth, it crossed the east–west Memphis & Charleston, and at Meridian, it connected with the Alabama & Mississippi River line. The Mobile & Great Northern Railroad was opened in November 1861. It ran from Tensas landing to Pollard, Alabama, where it linked with the Alabama & Florida—giving Mobile access to Montgomery and Pensacola. During the war, the largest single Confederate troop movement by rail (twenty-five thousand men) would come through Mobile.[7] The importance of Mobile's rail and water transportation was not lost on one Union general, who later noted that "[h]aving communication the year round by river as well as by the railroads into the heart of Alabama and Mississippi, it [Mobile] was regarded as one of the keys to the Confederacy."[8]

Considering all these facts, it is easy to understand why Mobile's residents were somewhat optimistic about their future. One writer spoke for many when he stated that "[w]e now venture the prediction that the city of Mobile in three years more of the toil, industry, public spirit and enterprise of its citizens, enter upon a new career of prosperity and development."[9] However, the events in the next four years—during which the United States would go through its most severe trial—would send the people of the port city along a very unpredictable course.

–LONNIE A. BURNETT

Preface

It has been more than 150 years since the events you are about to read took place in the old port city of Mobile, Alabama. Cotton was king in those days, and the city was still under Confederate charge. In many ways, the people who lived here thought differently about everything: slavery, women and their place in the home and what was considered good and right. Since it was among the last of the cities taken by Union forces, it experienced the greatest amount of change in the shortest amount of time.

Mobile has always been a uniquely southern city. To a large degree, this is a book about the people who lived in Mobile and their stories and experiences in one of the most turbulent times in its existence: from August 1864 to April 1865. While the history of this beautiful city is exhaustive, I can only focus this book on these eight months and the events surrounding them. It is my hope that this mixture of actual events and historical narrative will result in a solid academic base in which to begin a new conversation in research about the Civil War era. You will discover, like I did, the life and times of those who existed in a very troubled Mobile, Alabama.

The idea for this literary journey happened in the most unique fashion. I was digging though clippings files at the Minnie Mitchell Archives, located at Oakleigh Place in Mobile, Alabama, about three years ago. At least one brave archivist had collected a good amount of local information and organized it according to subject in standard gray filing cabinets. One would normally ignore such a feature in today's digital world, but the current archivist, Bob Peck, asked me to go through them. Like any good volunteer, I began opening each drawer and scanned the contents.

My training as a librarian kicked in, and my curiosity was piqued. There was so much wonderful data about Mobile and the surrounding area in newspaper clippings, letters and photos. There were folders containing information about streets, long-destroyed buildings and even the old trolley cars that use to run up and down Royal Street. It was quite amazing to see so much information in such a place. I have always loved history—why else would I volunteer at the archives?—but this collection was so much more than it seemed.

One day I came across a folder that interested me more than the others. It contained letters, newspaper clippings and original manuscripts on stories about Mobile. The stories in that manila folder were so personal and gave a new perspective on the Civil War experience. Why were they not published anywhere? Why were they hiding in this drawer, when they contained a fresh perspective on the war?

When I began reading the contents, I realized that they were mostly about the time after the Battle of Mobile Bay. This led me to a new question: Mobile did *not* fall at the Battle of Mobile Bay? I discovered that Mobile still remained in Confederate hands eight more months after that significant fight. Actually, Mobile fell to Union forces on April 12, 1865. This only led to more questions: What happened in the city during those solitary eight months? Why did it take so long? How important was Mobile to the Confederate and Union governments during this time?

As I began my research into this period, I soon discovered that a lot of things happened in the city of Mobile during this siege. I learned that while the city was in this odd holding pattern, it still contained whites, freed blacks, slaves, Jews and Creoles. All these different groups existed in Mobile while Union forces tried to close off the bay. The more information I found, the more I began to realize that this could actually be a book worth writing.

I am a government documents librarian at the University of South Alabama by trade, and my search skills and the library resources I had access to began to fill in the historical gap between August 1864 and April 1865. With government documents resting at my fingertips, I was able to build an actual account of the events during this time. I used these resources to gather information about the commanding generals, the military movements and the battles. Military warfare was never my strong suit, so this information was invaluable.

After utilizing government information, I also took advantage of publicly available digital collections and microfilm collections at both the University

Preface

of South Alabama and the Mobile Public Library Genealogical and Historical Collection. During this period of research, I kept my focus on discovering the people who lived in this city through this time. I wanted to know how they lived, what they did and what each day was like. I worked to get as close as possible to the time and tried to reflect this in the book. I do hope that I was successful.

Finally, I want to thank you for investing a little bit of your time into the lives of those you will meet as you read. My goal was to save them from becoming lost to history. Now you, too, will experience a little of Octavia's desperation after the death of her husband, Willie's fear as he runs from the blockaders and Joseph's awe of Mobile during the Civil War. In a unique way, we all thank you for investing in our words and proving that they do, indeed, matter.

Acknowledgements

It is often said that it takes a village to raise a child. I can honestly say that it took a wonderful group of people, my village of friends and family, to make this book happen. First and foremost, I would like to thank Jesus Christ for planting the dream of writing in my heart.

After him, I would like to give thanks to the weary souls who invested their time in me—giving a little of themselves to make this project happen. Beverly Russell and Mary Duffy, you are a gift to the English language. Your insight polished the rough edges. Beverly, I pray that Julia sees the treasure she has in a mother. Bob Peck, your dedication astounds me, and your love of keeping these treasures alive does not go unnoticed. Thank you for all your help.

Last, but never least, I would like to thank Dad, Mom and Don. In addition, I would like to thank my grandmothers, Elma Webb and Martha Wigstrom. You have endured your unique daughter and granddaughter well.

Chapter 1
A Prequel

Rumors of War

What constitutes a State?
Not high raised battlements, or labored mound,
Thick wall, or moated gate;
Not cities proud, with spires and turrets crown'd,
Nor bays, and broad-armed ports,
Where laughing at the storm, rich navies ride;
Nor starred nor spangled courts,
Where low brow'd absences wafts perfume to pride
No; men, high-minded men—
Men, who their duties know,
But know their rights, and, knowing, dare to maintain.[10]

Alabama made a dramatic move to become a Confederate state when it withdrew from the United States of America on January 11, 1861. Every county in the state wanted a voice for their concerns and sent representation to the Constitutional Convention held in Montgomery. The representatives from Mobile, a wealthy port city of thirty thousand residents, were John Bragg, E.S. Dargan, H.G. Humphries and Dr. George Augustus Ketchum. These Mobile delegates would be among the first to sign the ordinance to "dissolve the Union between the State of Alabama and other States."[11]

Edward Bloch, a Jewish boy living in Mobile at the time, was eight years old when Alabama separated from the Union: "I can…recall that amid the great rejoicings which followed the secession of Alabama and Virginia, on

Meeting of the Southern Confederacy in Montgomery, Alabama. *Courtesy of the Library of Congress.*

which occasion every house in the city was illuminated, party feeling ran so high that mobs threatened the occupants of any house that did not present candle-lit front window panes."[12]

Fort Morgan, Fort Gaines and the arsenal at Mount Vernon had fallen to rebel hands on January 4, 1861.[13] Alabama Legislature for the new Confederate state quickly passed an ordinance to protect Mobile from surprise attack and placed General Braxton Bragg in command of the city. His job was to design an impregnable defense for the city and bay. "When the works were in order, General Joseph E. Johnston pronounced Mobile the 'best fortified city in the Confederacy.'"[14]

The majority of the fighting during the Civil War existed to the north or to the east, and after three years, Alabama's borders had still not been breached or its defenses tested. Many of its residents felt a phantom sense of calmness and protection, especially in the culturally affluent Mobile. "There being no enemy in sight at the time, and nothing to fight, the members of the companies at these batteries (Hutchimon, Gladden, and McIntosh) which were composed of young men of Mobile, would pass away the time by entertaining the ladies at balls and parties that were given at these forts (Fort Morgan and Fort Gaines), the guests being transferred to and from the forts by large yawl boats."[15]

Right: General Braxton Bragg. *Courtesy of the Library of Congress.*

Below: Map of the defenses of Mobile. *Courtesy of the Library of Congress.*

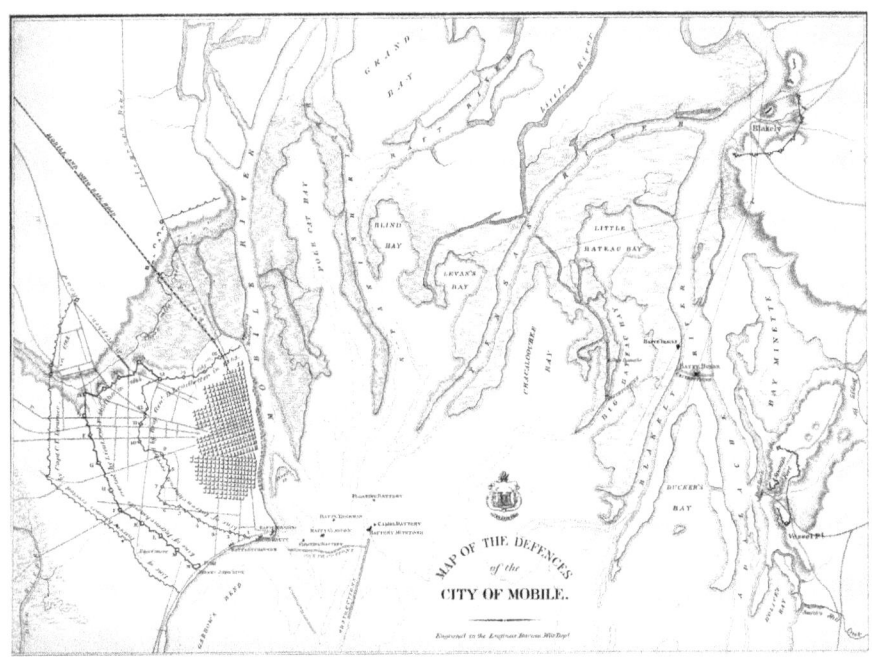

The cotton docks in Mobile, Alabama. *Courtesy of the Delaney Collection, History Museum of Mobile, compiled by Nick Beeson.*

Major General C.C. Andrews, of the Union army, commented, "Socially, politically and commercially, it (Mobile) resembled New Orleans (except that its commerce was smaller), and between the cities there was considerable cordiality. The liberalizing influence of commerce had tended to foster a fraternal and national spirit. Stephen A. Douglas had been welcomed there with enthusiasm in 1860 and received a large vote in the Presidential election."[16]

Mobile was not a cotton-raising county and did not have large plantations within its borders.[17] Mobile served as a port to transport much-needed supplies into the newly formed Confederate States of America and would continue to export goods using fast ships called blockade-runners until the Battle of Mobile Bay. Cotton, the universal currency, left Mobile ports for Havana, Cuba, and other countries beyond the Gulf of Mexico. In 1859, Mobile exported eight hundred thousand bales.[18] Selma, Alabama—a major supplier of battleships, guns and ammunition—shipped military supplies down the Alabama River to the Mobile River, through the port and out to other parts of the Confederacy. Mobile's port was second only to New Orleans and became the Confederacy's most important port after New Orleans was taken by Union forces in April 1862.[19]

The loss of New Orleans directly affected the city of Mobile. Thousands of people from New Orleans would join the number of refugees already living in the city when Union general Nathanial P. Banks ordered all those loyal to the Confederacy out of New Orleans. He wanted them out so desperately that he loaded them on a ship with the promise that it would take them directly to Mobile. The trip only went as far as Pascagoula, Mississippi, where the loyal rebels and their families were put to shore and ordered to get to Mobile any way they could. When the people of Mobile heard of this, they sent private carriages and wagons to bring them into the city. They remained in the city until the end of the war—put up in hotels and in the homes of local families.[20]

The wealth that had poured into the city previously and throughout the majority of the Civil War led to a cultural renaissance that could not be matched. Founded in the early 1700s by the French, Mobile was already a city known for gentility and refinement. Large mansions and grand houses lined the streets like jewels in Mobile's crown. A city of wealth always needs those to fill the service industry. In Mobile, middle-class whites, Jews, poor whites, mulattos, Creoles, free blacks and slaves filled those roles.

Miss Augusta J. Evans was a well-known author, staunch Confederate supporter and part of the Mobile melting pot. An intelligent, strong-willed southern lady, she was not afraid to speak her mind. Her opinion was expressed in many passionate letters she sent to Confederate leaders, commanders and the local newspapers.

An indication that she was not an average southern lady appeared early in her life. She wrote her first novel, *Inez*, in secret. Augusta's efforts at writing were discovered one morning by Minervy, a house servant owned by her father, Matt Evans. Instead of telling Augusta's father what his fifteen-year-old daughter was doing, Minervy, who often called Augusta "Gusta Jane," chose to help her hide the manuscript. Most servants like Minervy did remain faithful to their owners during the first two years of the Civil War but became restless during the final years.[21] Despite expectations, the relationship between Augusta and Minervy seems to have been a deep one and extended beyond that of owner/slave. Minervy remained with Miss Evans long after emancipation.

Augusta's book, *Inez*, was given to her father as a Christmas present. The once-hidden work somehow made it out of the hands of Augusta's father and into Harpers publishing house. The response must have been positive because not long after, the eighteen-year-old Augusta followed it with the largely successful *Beulah*. The first publication sold 2,200 copies during its

The home that Augusta Jane Evans purchased for her family from the royalties of her successful book, *Beulah*. Hardaway-Evans-Wilson-Sledge House, 2564 Spring Hill Avenue, Mobile, Alabama. *Courtesy of the Library of Congress.*

first year of publication. She used the money from her literary success to purchase a house in her beloved city, Mobile, Alabama, on Springhill Avenue for her family and herself.[22]

In February 1864, Miss Evans visited Columbia, South Carolina, probably to finish proofreading a copy of her latest work, *Macaria*. The venture was fraught with problems. Due to the threat of Union attack at Charleston, the publisher decided to move its presses to Columbus, Georgia. Augusta's efforts to finish this book would be worth it; *Macaria* would bring her wide fame.[23] After working diligently to get her book published, experiencing an unfamiliar city and the looming threat of Union attack so close, the only thing Miss Evans wanted to do was get back home to nice, safe Mobile.

What Miss Evans wanted to do and could do were two entirely different things. Her difficult time would continue as she tried to get back home to Mobile by train. Augusta shared with her close friend, Mrs. Rachel Lyons Heustis, "When we arrived at Montgomery [Alabama], we found that no ladies were allowed to leave that place en route for Mobile. I was fully resolved to come however at all hazards and so expressed myself to the Provost Marshal. He seemed very polite, but much puzzled, and finally gave me a passport to Mobile, on the express condition that as soon as I arrived, I would make all things satisfactory to General Maury, who had prohibited the return of non-combatants."[24]

Augusta then complained that when she got to Pollard, the provost marshal stalked into the ladies' train car and ordered everyone out. She showed her pass from Montgomery, but it did not work.[25] The charms that she had used to get her this far had ended. The marshal at Pollard told her that he had received peremptory orders from General Dabney Maury to stop all ladies. Obviously this did not satisfy Miss Evans, and as soon as she was able, she sent a telegraph to General Maury himself, regarding her situation. He replied the next day, making exception to his own direct orders to not allow any women back into the city and informing the command at Pollard to allow Miss Evans to come at once to Mobile. Of course, General Maury had more to be concerned about than the travels of Augusta Evans.

Even if Augusta Evans had known what was going on at Fort Powell during this same time she was struggling to get back into Mobile, it is a surety that she would have still insisted on going home. Fort Powell, sitting on top of a shallow oyster reef at Grant's Pass and only thirty miles south of the city, was shelled by the Union navy beginning on February 16, 1864; the bombardment did not cease until February 27, 1864. Despite the closeness of the shelling, many of those in Mobile still did not realize that danger was quickly coming closer to home. The *Macon Daily Telegraph* reported, "A friend who is familiar with the locality, says that nothing drawing over eight feet of water can get through Grants Pass into Mobile Bay."[26]

The residents continued to use the Shell Road, a road composed of oyster shells that ran alongside the city side of Mobile Bay for seven miles toward

Shell Road as it ran along Mobile Bay in the late 1800s and early 1900s. *Courtesy of the Minnie Mitchell Archives, Oakleigh House, Mobile, compiled by Robert Peck.*

the ocean. The view was excellent, and the wonderfully cool sea breeze made this drive a favorite for carriages and the courting couples that rode in them. At the end of this road "full of lovely country villas, unkempt hedges of Cherokee Rose, and arbors of Scuppernong grapes"[27] was a refreshment house where travelers could get a cool drink and a snack or two. One visitor to the city took the leisure trip down the Shell Road while the Union ships and Fort Powell were exchanging fire. He rather calmly stated that as he was enjoying the refreshment house and gazing out the windows toward Mobile Bay, "[w]hile the heavy Brooks gun in the fort fired it shook the windows so as to make them jingle."[28]

Everyone was confident in Fort Gaines and Fort Morgan protecting the initial passage in and out of Mobile Bay despite the vibrations felt beneath their feet and through their walls. Even high school students from Barton Academy, the oldest school in Alabama, did their part in building the fortifications of Fort Morgan. Frances Jane Mosby and other girls made sandbags that were piled high on the bastions of the fort during a holiday.[29] In addition, they were extremely confident in the city's defenses. "No persons of either sex or age scarcely paid attention to the notification of the Commanding General, so little is the concern of the Mobilians as to the boasted attack of the Yankees."[30]

Many people living in Mobile refused to leave, or if they did leave, they were quick to come back home when they felt it was safe. Augusta Evans returned home, like many others, on the next train out of Pollard, Alabama. "Many who did leave returned when its defense seemed assured, and once back home they were not so easily moved a second time." An editor facetiously wrote, "The Yankees are coming to Mobile and not now they ain't. But it is all the same to the people of Mobile. They have heard the cry of the wolf so often…that the recent outgivings…have produced no visible effect."[31]

There were assurances that Major General Dabney Maury was in control of a well-protected city. Dabney Herndon Maury was born on May 21, 1822, in Fredericksburg, Virginia, and he deeply loved all things in the South. He was the nephew of the renowned scientist Commodore Matthew Fontaine Maury. He tried to be a lawyer, but it really did not work out for him, and so he enrolled at West Point. His left arm was shattered by a musket ball during the Mexican-American War, resulting in permanent damage. They gave this adventurous man a desk job at West Point, as instructor, for five years.

When the Civil War began in May 1861, Maury could no longer settle for light duty. He turned in his resignation for the U.S. Army and returned to Richmond, Virginia, where he was commissioned as a captain in the Confederate army. After quickly rising in the ranks in the Western Theater at the Battles of Pea Ridge, Luka and Corinth, he was ordered to Mobile, Alabama, in 1863 to replace Major General Simon Bolivar Buckner as commander of the District of the Gulf.

Dabney Maury had a valid reason for giving the order to refuse to allow noncombatants back into the city of Mobile in February 1864. A report he wrote on February 15, 1864, told of an escaped prisoner from Pensacola, Florida, who reported that Farragut was there, preparing to attack Grant's Pass and that his fleet now lay off the bar of Mobile Bay.[32] The very same day, Admiral Farragut's forces began to open fire on Fort Powell. The next fifteen days would be filled with an assault that included more than two thousand mortar and cannon rounds, but the fort held its ground.

The command of Mobile was a rather calm experience for General Maury, but he realized that it was about to change. He explained in his report to the Confederate secretary of war that he just did not have enough men. Grant's Pass was very close to Mobile, and he had 10,000 men for the whole department; he would have only 8,300 men to protect Mobile, specifically. He stated that he should have an additional 6,000 to 7,000 troops to withstand a siege successfully. He had enough food to last for a while, but he was lacking ordnance supplies. He had no more than 250 rounds for each cannon, and while he knew it was difficult to get these items, this was an emergency.

General Maury had a daunting job. He could not get the noncombatants to leave for safer places, and getting additional troops sent to Mobile when the Confederate army was running short of manpower seemed impossible. The people in the city had grown used to the presence of the Federal fleet outside the bay. The confidence they held for the fortifications of the city only increased when one of the Federal vessels that tried to steam up near the mouth of the Fowl River struck a torpedo and became planted there. Almost everyone aboard that ship died.[33] The next best thing would be to build up Mobile's defenses.

The attempt to move women and children out of the city failed miserably. It was well known throughout the Confederacy that Mobile was considered one of the safest and most enjoyable cities. Maury could not even get Madame Octavia Walton LeVert, one of Mobile's most popular and colorful residents, to leave the city. Her home was located on the corner of Government and Royal Streets and was the focal point of Gulf Coast society even during those trying times. Despite the death of her husband, Dr. Henry LeVert, in March 1864, it is thought that she continued to host parties, despite wearing the black dress of those in mourning.[34]

The citizens of Mobile were still in the antebellum mindset, and while they knew that the War of the Rebellion was happening, their experiences of the war were only in pen and ink form—letters from loved ones fighting up north. Despite the assurances that towns located in a more northern part of the state would receive and provide support for evacuees, General Maury realized that the enemy would have to begin operations against Mobile before the civilians would leave. The people would have to experience the ground shaking from the blast of shells, the air filled with smoke from cannon fire and that deep feeling of desperation before they would begin taking one of the boats that traveled daily to Montgomery and farther north.

The trip to Montgomery was a short day's travel by steamboat. In many ways, it was the best city for evacuees. It had a lot going for it from the loyal Confederates' perspective. The residents of Montgomery were very receptive to helping Mobile evacuees find housing. A committee actually surveyed homes in the area to find places for them to stay and worked on providing provisions for those in need.[35]

An example of a dress a lady would wear in Mobile to attend parties and balls but still be in mourning for the loss of a loved one. *Courtesy of the Minnie Mitchell Archives, Oakleigh House, Mobile, compiled by Robert Peck.*

Those Mobilians who did leave continued to return home, especially after the shelling of Fort Powell had ceased and the Union forces retreated to regroup. "There are no movements of importance in the West or the South. Farragut is said to be still intent upon frightening the Mobilians, but thus far has not succeeded."[36]

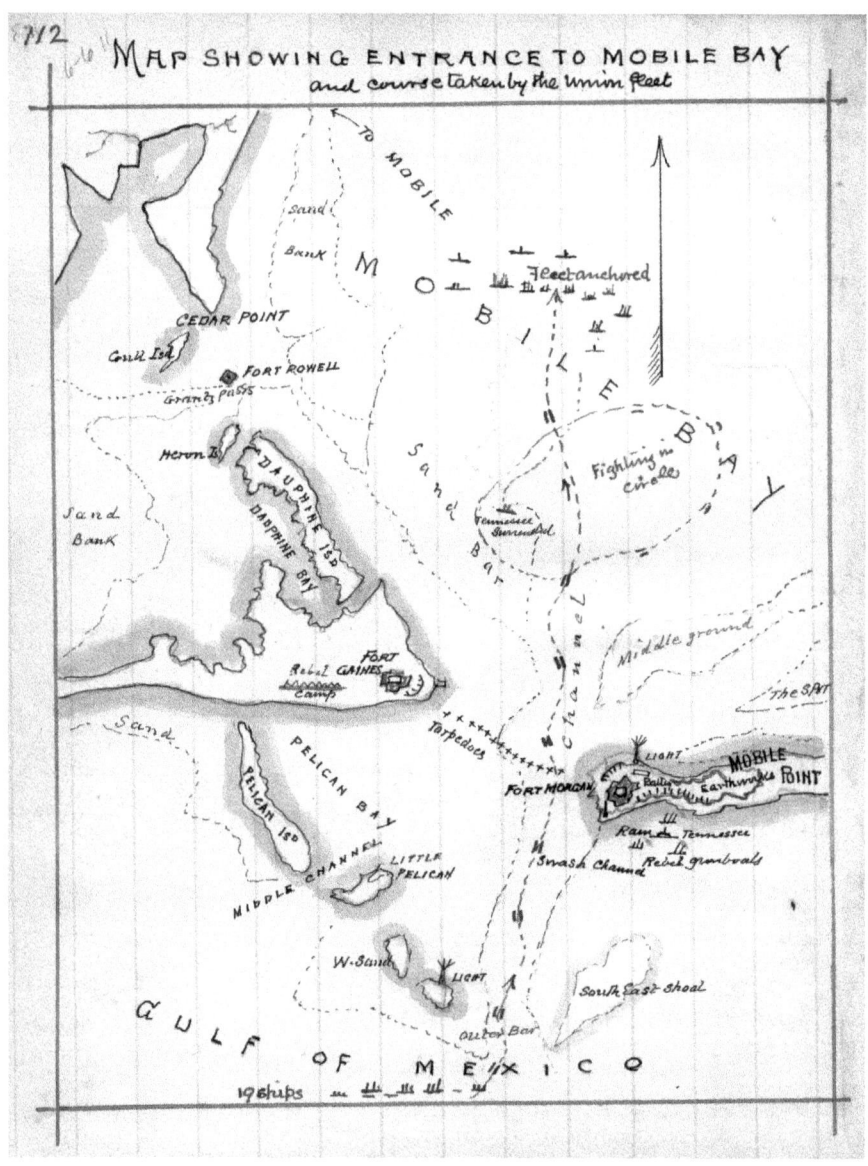

Fort Powell was only thirty miles to the south of Mobile. Robert Knox, *Map Showing Entrance to Mobile Bay and Course Taken by Union Fleet. Courtesy of the Library of Congress.*

In the coming months, this mindset would be considered short-sighted. In a matter of weeks, the feeling of protection and fearlessness would change to defenselessness and concern for tomorrow. The Yankees were finally coming for Mobile, and no one knew if it would stand.

Chapter 2

AUGUST 1864

Battle of Mobile Bay

So, when, from blazing ports,
Hurling at rebel forts
Cannon blows thunderous,
Down on Mobile he led,
While all the deep sea fled,
Quaking, from under us;
Where the blue rockets flashed,
Where the hot shell was dashed,
Where the shot madly crashed,
There we saw Farragut.[37]

A hot month, August 1864 brought sensational change, and the community felt the first tinges of fear. Entrepreneurial businessmen placed notices in the *Mobile Evening Telegraph*, offering to send off slaves to any part of the Confederacy.[38] Loyal Confederate ladies who remained in the city hid valuables in the hollowed legs of massive tables, chairs and trunks or buried them in the yards of their homes.[39] Mrs. Margaret Irwin buried her silver service in the backyard of Oakleigh Place, the Irwin family home during the Civil War.

Lieutenant Colonel James M. Williams, commander at Fort Powell, afraid for the safety of his wife and young son, sent them out of Mobile by one of the many steamboats traveling north, up to the Alabama River. "Under the pressure of the most serious of these alarms, many of our citizens sent

Oakleigh House in Mobile, Alabama. *Courtesy of the Library of Congress.*

their families to remote and safer places. Some of them, however, afterwards returned to the city and are now here returned under the extraordinary delusion that as these alarms were groundless, so if necessary must be all other alarms."[40] What would convince those die-hards who refused to leave the city to actually go? Maybe the fall of Fort Morgan and Fort Gaines would be the convincing factor.

On August 3, 1864, Rear Admiral David Farragut, who had captured New Orleans for the Union two years earlier, began the attack from the coast. Confederate general Maury continued to call on all men able to bear arms to enroll themselves in battle. "The greatest confidence prevails here," he declared.[41]

Miss Frances Jane Mosby wrote of the serene waters and Confederate gunboats, their sides protected with railroad iron, guarding the entrance into the Mobile River. She recalled small batteries resting throughout the bay and how they were manned by old men, boys and disabled soldiers originally sent to the city to recover from their wounds.[42]

Miss Mindenhall and Miss Mosby, two young ladies from wealthy families who chose to stay, were gathering figs for breakfast and were enjoying the morning meal when the anticipated Battle of Mobile Bay began. "We talked gaily over the happenings of a visit, made a day or two before, to a part of the earth works which had been built around the city. We discussed rifle pits, citadel and big guns, but this was more than interspersed by talk of the officers, who showed us around. I remember—and what trivial things we do remember at such times, that George, the dining room servant, passing the cornmeal battercakes to me just as the first stroke of the deep toned old Guard House bell rang out, stroke following stroke rapidly."[43]

The Guard House bell, off Government Street, was followed by the big Market Bell. The Market Bell, off Royal Street, was followed by the Cathedral Bell. Within five minutes, every bell in town was pealing strokes of alarm, a pandemonium of sound. Miss Mosby and her friend rushed to downtown Mobile by cab and were stopped at St. Francis Street:

> *The confusion was indescribable, but we soon learned the cause. At Sunrise that morning Admiral Farragut had formed his line of battle to attack the forts. The memorable and hard fought Battle of Mobile Bay was then in progress....Everybody seemed to have lost their heads. Confederate officers, of whom there seemed to be a good many, were hastily and forcibly trying to form squads of men, trying to drill them....Among a pushy, thronging crowd of men, women and negroes, I remember I noted the absence of children....I remember catching a glimpse of General Dabney Herndon Maury riding up the street doing all he could to get order out of chaos.*[44]

News of the morning fight, the sinking of the monitor USS *Tecumseh* and the events happening below the city were only half told by telegraph before the wires were cut. It left the crowd with a feeling of possible victory.[45] This could explain why four steamboats loaded with spectators, mostly ladies, traveled down to the forts to see the fight. Only when Union boats moved past the entrance into Mobile Bay did they run in haste back to the city.[46] Soon to follow was the Confederate navy gunboat CSS *Morgan*, the only rebel ship to survive the Battle of Mobile Bay. The *Mobile Evening Telegraph* remarked, "A spectator of the battle, who came up on the blockade running steamer *Mary*, says that ours fought with great spirit. He saw especially the maneuvers of the *Selma*'s Captain Pat Murphy, and describes them as beautiful and very effective."[47]

On August 6, the city conclusively learned of the loss of the CSS *Tennessee*, an ironclad ram that was to protect the forts, and the loss of Fort Gaines: "The *Tennessee* fought the enemy nobly for two or three hours, when she was obliged to succumb. Admiral Buchanan received a severe wound to the

The CSS *Selma*, one of the best Confederate ironclads in its navy. *Courtesy of the Dabney Collection, History Museum of Mobile, compiled by Nick Beeson.*

The CSS *Tennessee* fought hard in the Battle of Mobile Bay but lost to the USS *Hartford*. *Courtesy of the Library of Congress.*

leg.…Captain Johnston is safe. All of them are prisoners of war. The *Selma* was disabled and obliged to surrender."[48]

The Bay Shell Road, the ambling pleasure path along Mobile Bay, had dramatically changed its purpose in a matter of days. Mobilians and officers defending the city from Union attack traveled down the road by horse, by cab or on foot to where the vista of the bay was uninterrupted and the sailing ships

The U.S. frigate *Hartford. Courtesy of the Library of Congress.*

became clear. Farragut's own ship, the *Hartford* moved about, and the United States flag flew from its mast. One rebel officer commented, "That is the handsomest flag that ever waved, and the time was when I would have died in its defense—and even now, when it is red with our blood, I cannot shake off the old regard."[49]

The CSS *Morgan*, now safe behind Confederate water entrenchments, began firing its cannons toward the *Hartford*. "The *Hartford* rounded to and discharged a few guns in acknowledgement…and then quietly dropped down to an anchorage below. Her shots whistled by us and fell into the water far up towards the city."[50]

Major General Dabney Maury's telegraph to the War Office on August 6, 1864, contained disheartening news for J.A. Seddon, Confederate secretary of war: "Seventeen of the enemy's vessels—four ships and three ironclads—passed Fort Morgan this morning.…The *Tennessee* surrendered after a desperate engagement with the enemy fleet.…The *Selma* was captured. The Gaines was breached near the hospital. The *Morgan* is safe, and will try to run up tonight. The enemy's fleet has approached the city. A monitor has been engaging Fort Powell all day."[51]

In Mobile, the loss was devastating. A gentleman offered a $500 Confederate bill for $10 in gold but could not get anyone to do the exchange or even to make an offer. On that day, the price of everything went up to double the prices of the previous exorbitant rates.[52]

The naval fight between the *Hartford* and the *Tennessee*. "Great Naval Victory in Mobile Bay, Aug. 5th 1864." *Courtesy of the Library of Congress.*

Fort Morgan was now in Union sights, and Fort Powell, the small battery located at Grant's Pass, was to help defend it. How well Lieutenant Colonel James M. Williams stood his ground against the Union gunboat USS *Chickasaw* would later come into question by military trial.

The loss of the forts and the dismay felt in the city led Mayor R.H. Slough, perhaps on the steps of the Customhouse, where the Confederate military and engineering department was housed, to issue a proclamation. He called for the people of Mobile to stand and not lose heart but to also increase the thing they were lacking: men to fight. He stated, "We must gather every man fit for defense into some organized body, and hold ourselves in readiness to repel attack, come from what quarter it may. This is the only way to make our efforts useful, and to stand strong against the progress of the foe, in case he should approach us within reach of the weapons that we have at command."[53]

Union forces had breached the entrance to Mobile Bay, but this was not the end of the defenses protecting the Mobile River, nor the city of Mobile. The *Macon Daily Telegraph* explained in its August 8 edition:

> *To satisfy our readers who, through ignorance of the defenses of Mobile, may be apprehensive of our ability to hold the city, now that the Federal*

> *fleet has passed the forts, we would mention that Forts Morgan and Gaines are not the only defenses that protect the city on the water. Nearer to the town, and right across the bay, is a cordon of batteries, several of them iron-clad and all regarded as powerful works. They are so constructed that their fire bears upon each other, thus effectually preventing the enemy from attempting to board and carry them by storm. Besides these works we have two iron-clad floating batteries which can perform effective service. If the water defenses of Mobile are manned by brave and determined men we do not fear the result.*[54]

The newspapers were certain that Mobile would stand, and they were just as certain that Fort Morgan would fall. The enemy's ships soon began firing wildly at the fort.[55] Fort Gaines had fallen to Union forces, and Fort Morgan was only three miles away by sea. It would, no doubt, put up a fight. The fort was well provisioned, and it was quite able to hold out against any force the Federals could bring. However, the position of the fort in the bay, surrounded by Union forces, made it incapable of withstanding a siege.

The once firmly Confederate sympathies of the people of Mobile became divided into two parties, one part for war and the other for peace. "The war faction is composed of about one-third of the people, who have expressed the determination to burn the city, if they have to evacuate it."[56]

It was believed that the line of water batteries blocking Union forces from the city were placed out so far that the city could not be shelled.[57] Others were quick to give their advice:

> *If the city is even shelled, it must make no difference. We would rather see every house in Mobile a heap of ashes than the federals in possession of it. There is absolutely no necessity for it to fall, if the Alabamians will perform their duty in a spirit worthy of their brothers and our cause. Twenty thousand men can be obtained from the militia and will be by the veteran troops of the Confederacy....Mobile must not exhibit less patriotism than Petersburg, Richmond, and Atlanta, and we believe that her people will show themselves awake to the dangers of the hour and act in a manner worthy of themselves and their liberties.*[58]

Heavy firing began at Fort Morgan on August 9 and continued for three days. Union forces managed to cut the telegraphic wire between the city and the fort. The shores of the bay, once beautiful and without blemish, were covered with the debris of the vessels lost in the recent engagements at the forts. The USS *Brooklyn*, USS *Hartford*, two monitors and four other ships lingered in the bay within sight of Mobile docks. The air was smoky from the large amounts of tar, pitch and turpentine burned along the docks to keep the Federals from capturing it.[59] Confederate troops, rallied by the loss of Fort Gaines, began arriving daily in the city.

Yet another plea was made for all private citizens to leave the city: "The General in command here, we learn, has received information that there is a probability that the city will be subjected to a bombardment next week, from the water side."[60] Housing arrangements were made in Greenville, Alabama, for evacuees: "At Greenville, houses for 5000 people have been erected for the express accommodation of refugees. It is a healthy country, there is abundance of good water, and no expense for rent. Any family can go there by applying to some member of the Safety Committee."[61]

One can assume that General Maury wished the citizens would leave Mobile as fast as Lieutenant Colonel Williams and his men abandoned Fort Powell. Maury and the local newspaper editor, John Forsyth, both felt that Lieutenant Colonel Williams left Fort Powell entirely too soon and that if it had held, the Union fleet would have been forced back out to sea and the harbor would be manageable without the gunboats. General Maury reported, "Colonel Williams should have fought his guns. They were not more exposed than those on every wooden ship, and vigorously served would probably have compelled the monitor to haul off."[62]

Instead, Colonel Williams's decision to abandon the fort left an entrance open for the enemy and invited a land attack directly on the city. There was an immediate call for Colonel Williams's report of events to be made public, hoping that it would vindicate his military conduct and save him from condemnation. It was a surprise that someone who had defended the position so well back in February could follow it up with a failure so great. It resulted in

John Forsyth. *Courtesy of the Delaney Collection, History Museum of Mobile, compiled by Nick Beeson.*

Colonel Williams being relieved of his command and placed under arrest.[63] A trial would follow in Mobile.

Despite the fall of Fort Gaines and Fort Powell to Union forces, Fort Morgan still stood against the heavy bombardment. The noise and vibration of the bombing could be heard in the city, but many were unaware of events at the fort since the telegraph wires had been cut below Fish River. Fort Morgan was still able to fire at ships in the deep channel that flowed just outside its walls, the main channel into Mobile Bay, and no one saw any of the Union ships approach the city again since the fall of Fort Gaines. Mobile was prepared for the worst, an attack on the city, and expected it any day. General Maury's call for reinforcements was being heard, and soldiers were arriving in the city or were on their way. Everyone felt certain and was most assured that the Yankees could do nothing on land; instead, it was shelling from the ironclads they feared.[64]

On August 15, 1864, the realities of the war came even closer to Mobile. The evening was greeted with two monitors and five gunboats crossing the Dog River bar, quickly discounting the reliance on the natural obstacles in the bay, and coming within miles of the obstructions sunk in Mobile Bay. These obstructions prevented the Union forces from traveling up the Mobile River and into the heart of Alabama. The ships opened fire for three hours on the formidable, floating Confederate batteries and gunboats, but did not do any damage. One of the Confederate gunboats "replied back handsomely,"[65] and the Union ships left at sunset. They could hear the sound of firing in the direction of Fort Morgan, so the people of Mobile felt certain that they were still embroiled in a fight.

Not everyone sat by anxiously waiting to hear of the fall of Fort Morgan; some decided to take matters into their own hands. On August 18, possibly distraught over the loss of Fort Powell or maybe attempting to prove himself, a man called Captain Moore, with the Creole Scouts of Mobile, took a skiff down to Cedar Point and managed to capture a Union lieutenant and eight others. He led all the prisoners back to the city with no problems.[66]

Spirits in the city of Mobile seemingly became a bit more positive after this capture, for on the same day the *Mobile Advertiser and Register* made a daring declaration, "Any man who will bet drinks in any subject at the present time of high prices must be absolutely certain of winning. The *Mobile Advertiser and Register* man offers to 'bet drinks' that his city does not fall into the hands of the Yankees this war. We do not notice this, Mr. Advertiser, to take you up. Oh no, not we."[67]

On August 24, the *Mobile Register* still felt confident that Fort Morgan would remain in Confederate hands despite Farragut's efforts to shell and

Fort Morgan just after the surrender. *Courtesy of the Library of Congress.*

starve it into submission. "He has invested in it on the land side and flung a few shots and shells at it from the fleet, just as he did at Fort Gaines, but does not find the same facile material to deal with. General Page is not a man to surrender a strong work on a speculation that he will not be able to hold it. He thinks it time enough to experiment. Had this rule governed, we believe that Forts Powell and Gaines would still be in our hands."[68]

By the end of this same day, the *Mobile Evening Telegraph* would report a different story:

> *Yesterday morning until afternoon, there was very heavy cannonading at Fort Morgan, and scouts who came in this morning report that it was in possession of the enemy. There are numerous rumors in respect of it, some of them not worth putting in type. It was said that the Yankee flag was seen over the works, but this needs corroboration. It is more positively stated that a Yankee gunboat was at the fort wharf, and others were seen moving in close proximity to it. At all events, the firing has ceased. We think it may be concluded that the fort is gone, but of any particulars in regard to it there is no news within the city.*[69]

Despite the desperate fight to keep Fort Morgan in Confederate hands, Union general Farragut sent the following report to his commodore: "Fort Morgan makes an unconditional surrender at 2pm today to the forces of the army and navy. Page did not make us wait as long as expected. We will cheer our flag and salute it, when hoisted, with one hundred guns, by the fleet."[70]

Word of the final fall of Fort Morgan reached the city on August 25, by a flag of truce boat that arrived at the docks. People began evacuating the city, up the Mobile and Alabama Rivers and by train, to Montgomery, but they were now being met with a negative response when they finally got there. "In all charity…we would advise those in quest of domiciles to spread out into the country, as being cheaper, healthier, and, in short, in every respect preferable, to the city."[71]

While those in Mobile followed these close events with great apprehension, they refused to let the defeat of the forts be a reason for distress: "So far as the defense of Mobile is concerned, the loss of 'Fort Morgan' amounts to nothing material, after 'Gaines' and 'Powell' had passed into the hand of the enemy."[72]

By August 27, the Yankees had landed troops at Cedar Point, the southernmost point of land in Mobile, but the chances of their troops traveling much farther were slim. Mobile had the time to build up the city's defenses, and this expected path was now full of entrenched Confederate soldiers.

While the city of Mobile was under a surreal act of war, in many ways things continued as if there were no war at all. The capture of runaway slaves was an almost daily occurrence. On August 28, just three days after the fall of Fort Morgan, black men from Tennessee, Mississippi, north Alabama and Kentucky were held in the Mobile County Jail until "[h]is owner come forward, prove property, pay jail fees and charges and take him away, or will be dealt with as the law directs."[73]

Even with the Union forces so close, the people in the city struggled to hold on to the cultural life they once knew. A Mr. W.H. Crisp had returned to the city and opened the Mobile Theatre, which "engaged an elegant and talented number of ladies and gentlemen as the members of the company."

Meanwhile, six Union vessels rested off Dog River bar from the morning to the evening of August 30. The forts were lost, so the only protection the city now had were shallow waters and the batteries in the upper bay preventing the Union ironsides from entering the Mobile river system.

"Mobile, as yet untouched, guarded by her shallow waters, her intricate lagoons amid her marshes, went back into its daily life, carrying into it the dull pain of expectancy—and waited—waited till the sealing of the inevitable. Days grew into weeks, weeks into months," said Fannie Jane Mosby.[74]

Chapter 3

SEPTEMBER 1864

Siege Begins

*And when the church bells' solemn chime
Floats on the evening air;
With humble hearts we offer up
This solemn fervent prayer.
Most Holy Father, gracious God,
Thy chastening rod we feel,
Submissive here we humbly ask,
Protect our loved Mobile.*[75]

Atlanta had fallen to Federal forces.[76] In U.S. dollars, $100 in gold now equaled $3,000 in Confederate money.[77] A lady, claiming to have buried money at an old earthwork just outside Mobile, lost it all when "a gang of hands" discovered it and split it among themselves.[78] Runaway slaves were hunted by patterollers[79] through remote, dangerous places such as Three Mile Creek Swamp, trying to reach Union forces presumably at Cedar Point.[80]

On September 1, the *Mobile Advertiser and Register* reported, "One of the monitors cruising in the upper bay, got aground yesterday about one mile below the obstructions, where she remained at dark. She fired a shell at one of our batteries which fell far short of the object."[81] It was clear that Union shells could not reach the city. The officials in Mobile could now take a moment to breathe. After the threat of invasion; the rush of soldiers in the city; and the battle raging at Fort Morgan, Fort Gaines and Fort Powell, September 1864 was quiet.

Colonel Williams, accused of abandoning Fort Powell, wrote to his wife on September 2 about what transpired: "It is all over and as I always assured you, I have been acquitted of all blame in the Fort Powell affair. I return to my command today."[82] Williams was released from military arrest and was to resume his command, but this would not be the end of his struggle to clear his name. General Dabney Maury disliked the decision made in the trial and took it to his superior, Lieutenant General Richard Taylor, in charge of the Department of Alabama, Mississippi and East Louisiana. General Taylor, a close friend of General Maury, almost immediately suspended Williams until a decision could be made by the Confederate War Department.[83]

During this time, efforts to defend the city of Mobile increased drastically. Six to eight Union blockaders rested just below the Dog River bar on a daily basis.[84] Everyone was very aware of their position, but they were ignored by Mobile citizens as their daily life resumed. In a span of weeks, life was as it always had been for Mobile's elite and working-class population—minus a few luxuries, they endured the typical hot and wet weather common in Mobile in early September.

The well-to-do families were determined to maintain their lavish lifestyles. An actress, Miss Nellie Taylor, held a benefit play titled *Richelieu*.[85] The board of school commissioners at Barton Academy made arrangements for school to reopen in October.[86] Judson Female Institute offered boarding to female students that would take them away from the threat of danger in Mobile: "It will be seen that full provision has been made for instruction in all the departments of a thorough and polite education."[87] The markets in town were still well supplied with meats and vegetables, and the prices were stable.[88]

Surprisingly, fashion was becoming a concern for ladies, and they voiced this to the *Mobile Advertiser and Register*:

> *Will you not for the benefit of some of your country friends devote a small portion of your time and space to "the Fashions?" We all wear homespun dresses and home-made hats, but do not like to be entirely out of the fashion, if we are almost out of the world; we are deprived of many a little trip to the Gulf City on account of our old timey clothes. There are no beaux here to catch, but a few of our brave soldiers get a short leave of absence sometimes, to visit their friends, and of course we all wish to dress as becomingly as we can.*[89]

Augusta Evans was not fazed by the Union ships that sat in Mobile Bay, the sudden influx of Confederate fighters in the city or the threat of attack.

Barton Academy, the school for children in Mobile, remained open during the Civil War. Barton Academy, Government Street, Mobile, Alabama. *Courtesy of the Library of Congress.*

Instead, she had busied herself with more personal matters. She had taken a train to Columbus, Georgia, to collect her sick brother, Howard, who was injured in battle as a part of the Third Alabama Regiment. Her brother was treated by Dr. J.F. Heustis, who was engaged to her best friend, Rachel Lyons. When Augusta wrote to her of how well the young doctor had cared for her brother, she could not help but strongly encourage her friend to marry the doctor and move to Mobile before "the close of this seemingly endless war."⁹⁰

While Augusta Evans had only just started to feel the strain of war, Octavia Walton LeVert was a Mobile socialite who had felt that same strain consistently from the start of the Civil War. She had prevailed as the queen of Mobile society over the last thirty years. She was the most internationally known lady in the city, with Union and Confederate friends, but the war had changed her reputation and circumstances.

Octavia Walton LeVert was born near Augusta, Georgia, in 1810. She was the granddaughter of George Walton Sr., a signer of the Declaration of Independence, and the daughter of George Walton Jr., who was territorial secretary under General Andrew Jackson. Mr. Walton Jr. moved the entire family to Mobile in 1835, and Octavia married Dr. Henry S. LeVert in 1836. Octavia was opposed to the Alabama secession from the United States, but she remained with her husband in the city and was known to be very kind to the Confederate soldiers and their families in Mobile.⁹¹ When her husband died in March 1864, she found herself alone with her daughters in a city that viewed her more as a tolerated Unionist than a loyal Confederate.

An example of this altruism happened in July 1864, when Colonel Williams met Octavia for the first time. He observed:

Octavia LeVert. *Courtesy of the History Museum of Mobile, compiled by Nick Beeson.*

> *She is very interesting, yet somehow I cannot talk to her without an odd indefinable feeling of pity—She talks loyally enough—though by all accounts she has not always been sound in her devotion to our cause and for*

all I know may not be now. Poor old woman! There it is like a flash! I now know why I pity her—because she is old—she should be young and handsome and rich and then how firmly she would grasp the scepter which is slipping away from her hands everyday—she would then be the royal woman—now it is hard to believe she is anything but an old quack pretender.[92]

The lives of blacks, both free and slave, could not have been more different than that of the LeVerts and the Evanses, but like many wealthy Mobilians, they were a sustaining part of their lives. Free blacks and hired slaves did a variety of skilled jobs in the city. They were bricklayers, blacksmiths, house servants, draymen, steamboat hands, stevedores and dock workers.[93] Many of these men were forced to provide the physical labor to build the fortifications to protect the city: "From the beginning of the war, slaves from the town and surrounding areas were used in preparing the defenses of Mobile Bay, and even greater demands were made on them to fortify the port's harbor in the summer of 1864, after the Confederate Impressment Act of 1863."[94] In an effort to manage the fluctuating number of slaves in town, all slaves had to be at their homes after eight o'clock at night. Patterollers, the slave nickname for slave patrols, enforced this curfew.[95]

Still slaves, house servants in Mobile homes had a much better situation and saw no need to run away and face the patterollers. Nurses for children were usually girls about fifteen years old[96] and not uncommon in the city. Oakleigh Place, as a representation, owned by the Irwin family, had a well-beloved house servant by the name of Celie. She was the nursemaid for T.K.

The receipt for the purchase of two slaves in Mobile, Alabama. *Courtesy of the Minnie Mitchell Archives, Oakleigh House, Mobile, compiled by Robert Peck.*

House servant in Mobile, Alabama. *Courtesy of the Minnie Mitchell Archives, Oakleigh House, Mobile, compiled by Robert Peck.*

Irwin and Mary K. Irwin's children, Frank and Daisy.[97] She stayed with the family and took care of the children as they moved around the city during the Civil War. She would remain with the family in various household offices until she died.

With Union forces just a few miles away and the promise of freedom so close, some slaves thought that the risk of becoming a runaway was worth it. One owner placed this ad: "$250 Reward. Runaway from my place near Howards, Eastern Shore, my boy William, age 36…He has a wife owned by Mr. R.M.G Weatherford at Montgomery Hill, Baldwin County, AL. I think he will attempt to get his wife, and then induce her to go with him to the Yankee fleet."[98]

Slaves were not the only inhabitants trying to escape the city by reaching Federal forces. There was a desperate need for more men to fight for the Confederacy. The Confederate Conscription Act of 1862 was originally not given a lot of worry if one could get a pass, but the loss at the Battle of Mobile Bay turned Unionists in Mobile into hunted men.[99] One refugee made it to New Orleans and told his story to a local paper: "He had been for several days past been concealed in the swamps near Mobile, where there are still many others endeavoring to evade conscription.…The most complete military despotism is ruling in Mobile, no open difference of opinion being tolerated; and to attempt to criticize the acts of the military rulers will cost a man his liberty, and not infrequently, his life."[100]

General Dabney Maury, trying to protect the city, took the bold step of inviting Confederate general Nathan Bedford Forrest to Mobile to take a few days of rest and to send down one of his brigades as well:[101] "I thought that the enemy on hearing, as he surely would, that Forrest and his command were in Mobile, would delay the attack then under consideration. My wife wished to entertain him, and gave him a dinner, inviting some lady friends who were desirous of meeting this great hero."[102]

It is clear from the September 11 edition of the *Mobile Advertiser and Register* that General Forrest was not the only one General

Confederate general Nathan Bedford Forrest. *Courtesy of the Library of Congress.*

Maury invited to Mobile: "We have now in our city Lieutenant General Dick Taylor, Major General Maury, Major General Forrest, Major General Frank Gardner, Brigadier General Liddell, Brigadier General Nabers, Brigadier General Higgins, and Brigadier General Thomas. Governor Thomas H. Watts is also in the city."[103]

The middle of September's weather was still extremely warm, and the first signs of scarcity were showing. The city market still had a good supply of meat, but vegetables were becoming scarce.[104] The siege of the city was slowly beginning to take effect on the families who chose to remain in the city.

As if to taunt those in Mobile, the former Confederate gunboat CSS *Selma*, which sank in the Battle of Mobile Bay, was raised by Union forces and was seen shelling the woods near the mouth of the Dog River. They were also able to raise the gunboat CSS *Gaines* (taking it close to one of the shore batteries), fired a few shots and retired.[105]

Colonel Williams, of the Fort Powell affair, still felt that he had no choice in abandoning the fort and took the court-martial one step higher by appealing directly to Secretary of War James A. Seddon. He pleaded with Seddon, "In the name of Justice, and as a soldier of the Confederacy, whose honor is dear to him, and who has no other resort" for a speedy revision of his case."[106]

Over the course of the war, Mobile's value to the Confederacy grew almost daily. As battles were lost farther north, Mobile's key railroad lines, one major route to the interior of the Confederate government, had to be protected. Much of the military and the citizens felt that there would not be an attack from the Union forces in the area until the spring, winter never being the best time to fight. This would give General Maury much-needed time to build up forces in the city. Confederate general Richard Taylor advised Maury to fortify defenses on the eastern side of Mobile Bay, Spanish Fort and Fort Blakeley. "It was a great comfort to find an able officer in this responsible position, who not only adopted my plans, but improved and executed them," he remembered.[107]

The end of September saw the weather dramatically change, as is often the case in Mobile, from extreme heat to chilling cold. Mayor Slough was very aware of the lack of wood for cook fires and home hearths, both large and small. He began to seek contracts with businesses to help reduce the price of wood for the poor.[108]

A storm blew through Mobile during the last week of September, possibly a small hurricane, causing many operations of any kind to come to a standstill.[109] The final week of September saw an unexpected and unwelcome

Runaway slave hiding in a swamp. *Courtesy of the Library of Congress.*

problem: runaway slaves were flocking to Mobile, the quickest route to reach the Federals and freedom.

Slaves were entering the bay and swimming between Battery Buchanan, located in the city, and the new racetrack, about four miles south, trying to reach the Federal fleet:

> *Now let me suggest the almost utter impossibility for a negro to escape from Mobile or its vicinity, unless they do so from some point embraced within the above shore lines, and when we know this fact, and consider how many thousands slaves there are of our own, as well as those who have been sent to us from the interior to work on our fortifications, does it not occur to you that immediate attention should be given to this matter?...Why, it's within my own knowledge that not less than twenty-five valuable slaves belonging to parties residing around the Bay, have gone in the last few days. Many of them are very intelligent, and know every foot of ground between the city and Dog River, and can not only give much information to the enemy, but can be used by them as decoys and come ashore in the night time and incite discontent among other slaves, and be the cause of mischief....It might be argued that it would require boats. No such thing. The enemy's launches are prowling about in the Bay at all hours of the night, and nothing would be easier at many points that I could suggest than that negroes may wade out and get into them.*[110]

Only three miles away by water in Mobile Bay, the people of Mobile could no longer deny the Union presence in their world. They were beginning to feel the strain of the blockade and the small losses they were experiencing; they started to wonder what else they might lose. Before it was all said and done, would the loss be worth the present struggle?

Chapter 4

OCTOBER 1864

Freedoms Sacrificed

Furl that Banner, for 'tis weary;
Round its staff 'tis drooping dreary;
Furl it, fold it, it is best;
For there's not a man to wave it;
And there's not a sword to save it;
And there's not one left to lave it;
In the blood which heroes gave it;
And its foes now scorn and brave it;
Furl it, hide it—let it rest.[111]

October was stilled in Mobile,[112] much like the previous month. General John Bell Hood challenged Union forces around Decatur, Alabama.[113] The weather in Mobile was becoming more cool than warm. The price of shoes had risen to as much as $150 per pair.[114] Theft of a slave, horse, mare or mule; burglary; arson; and other crimes became punishable by hanging or ten years in prison, depending on the discretion of the jury.[115]

Yankee ships watched as Confederate ironclads placed torpedoes in the channel above Fort Morgan.[116] As the Confederacy lost major battles farther north, protecting the interior waterways became imperative. Mobile's location, at the mouth of the Alabama River system, was "composed of the great rivers, Tombigbee, Black Warrior, Cahaba and the Alabama, the last of which has for its most northern feeder the Coosa River, which rises in the

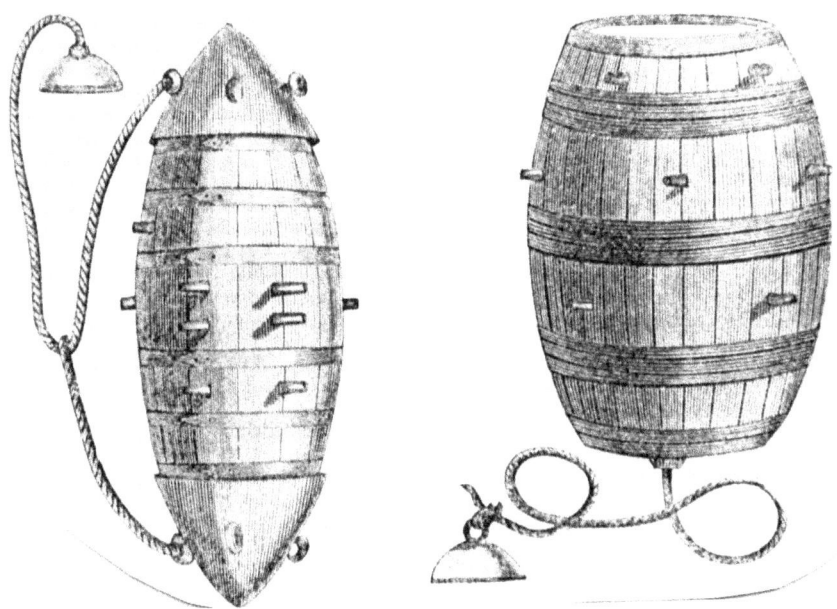

Confederate torpedoes. *Courtesy of the Delaney Collection, History Museum of Mobile, compiled by Nick Beeson.*

state of Georgia."[117] Were Union forces to get past the bay, the Confederacy would be dead before the end of the year.

Slaves still struggled to reach the Union ships in Mobile Bay, some making the ultimate sacrifice. On October 4, three runaways were found, drowned, near the Bay Shell Road. "They were no doubt drowned in attempting to get to the Yankee fleet."[118] Some slaves did not make it to the Union side in Mobile Bay, but others did manage a successful escape. Joseph Howard, a black solder captured by Confederates near Athens, Alabama, was marched on foot to Mobile. "There he had to work digging fortifications with impressed slaves. He said the Confederates enforced work discipline through whippings with a lash and fed him poorly with corn bread and mule meat." Howard was able to make his escape to a Union gunboat and later return to his army unit.[119]

Trains resumed on the Mobile & Ohio Railroad system, and a very important passenger train made its way to the city.[120] "The…train on Wednesday was freighted with 568 'American citizens of African descent,' recently captured by Forrest in north Alabama."[121] They were part of the 106th, 110th and 111th United States Colored Troops. Their names, their owners and the town they came from were published in the *Mobile Advertiser and Register*. Maury's intent was not to return the slaves to their masters.

Rather, those masters were invited to "receive the pay due them" for their slaves' labor.[122]

On October 17, of the group brought down from Tennessee, eighty black soldiers escaped the warehouse where the engineering department had them quartered.[123] It would not have taken them too long to figure out how to reach Union forces and regain their freedom. Some of the escaped soldiers were captured, but a number of them did get free.

In early October, five Union vessels sat off the Dog River bar. Two shots were fired from the batteries, and one shot was returned from the fleet.[124] Four foreigners and one black man were captured as they were trying to escape to the Yankees.[125] Foreigners in the city had a long history of trying to avoid becoming a part of the Confederate army. With more than half of Alabama's total foreign-born population living in Mobile and the city in danger of Union attack, the commanders needed these men. Finally, after exhausting all means to avoid conscription, the foreign-born men in the city offered to leave the port:

> *This method seldom proved satisfactory, since, in the few cases where the potential conscript was able to secure permission to leave the port, the United States blockading officers refused to cooperate, and in those cases where the blockaders would grant passage, the Mobile authorities would not cooperate. When the British Consul attempted to solve the dilemma by helping foreigners to escape, he was dismissed by the British Minister in Washington for his pains.*[126]

Southern Unionists, who could see the war ending soon, were desperate to escape conscription and prevent their children from being forced to join the Confederate army. William Rix's son, Willie, was fast approaching his sixteenth birthday. Determined to keep his son out of the war, he temporarily sent his son into hiding in the woods that surrounded the city. He consulted a friend, "Captain Merchant," who told him of a blockade runner that could smuggle Willie out of Mobile, but it was fraught with danger. "Blockade-running had become an art, like card-playing and other games of chance, and many a fortune was made and perhaps as many lost."[127] Rix was willing to take the chance, as he was desperate to keep his son out of the war. Willie would have to wait until the time was right for escape, and Captain Merchant would send a carriage when a ship was ready.[128]

The second week of October would be the birth of truly cold weather in the area. October 8 was a blustery day, causing people to transition from

Blockade running in Mobile Bay. "*Pocahontas* Capturing Blockade Runner *Antonia*." *Courtesy of the Library of Congress.*

their summer attire to their warmer clothes. It was the first cold weather of the season. The markets still had plenty of meats and vegetables, but their prices were becoming outrageously high. Flour was selling for more than $100 per sack.[129]

On October 10, the Federal fleet came too close to the Eastern Shore, and a Confederate battery opened fire. "Our citizens were aroused by the discharge of heavy guns in the bay....We are glad to say that we could hear of no damage to our forces, and that it is believed that the gunboats of the enemy were several times hulled."[130]

The *Mobile Advertiser and Register* reported that the attack on Mobile was abandoned on October 15: "Admiral Farragut is about to be transferred to the command of the North Atlantic blockading squadron, and Admiral Lee to succeed Farragut in command of the fleet in Mobile Bay, from which we infer that the attack on Mobile is to be abandoned."[131]

The report of Farragut leaving the area perhaps contributed to a gala atmosphere in the city:

> *Mobile, it seems to me, though I write it sorrowfully, is one vast bed of corruption—a kin to Gomorrah of old. I think it surpasses Richmond in the vastness of its pollution, number of "hells" and abodes of "flashy vice."*[132] *Young officers, who could get free passes to go to the city, would come to get relief from the war. There were receptions, parties and balls where they met those ladies still in Mobile. At these fashionable gatherings the gentlemen, as a rule, wore homespun, and*

the ladies dresses that has been turned and "adapted," perhaps several times over.[133]

Mayor Robert Slough, despite Governor Thomas H. Watts's order to close the bars, allowed "the city bar rooms to retail with open doors…all saloons were thrown open, and will so remain until further notice." The newspaper joked, "Who's agwine to gin a treat?"[134]

Many were quick to criticize the actions of the women in Mobile, who continued the festive environment despite the conditions of the soldiers in the field defending the Confederacy. The evacuees from New Orleans still remained in the city and helped to foster the festive atmosphere: "Mobile was called the Paris of the Confederacy, New Orleans having fallen so early in the fray, and gay indeed it was."[135] While many felt that all the dances, parties, band concerts and parades were unnecessary, others felt that it was a service that Mobile was able to provide for the soldiers and sailors stationed in the city.[136] Many men who came to Mobile seeking relief from the war ended up finding wives as well.[137]

An example of an event or celebration in Mobile, Alabama. *Courtesy of the History Museum of Mobile, compiled by Nick Beeson.*

One group of Kentuckians, members of the famous Orphan Brigade, snuck out of camp to get a meal of Mobile's famous oysters at the Battle House. "The men found themselves face to face with their brigade commander as they entered the Battle House. To their excuse that they were looking for stragglers, Colonel R.P. Trabue observed, '…you are looking for straggling oysters. I know what you are up to.'"[138]

In addition to getting leave to visit the city, soldiers were also sent to Mobile to recover from wounds acquired in battle. The medical facilities in the city benefited the people living in Mobile and the soldiers. The number of medical facilities in the city increased dramatically. "The Confederate authorities constructed…at least seven new hospitals for soldiers and sailors."[139] The Sisters of Charity, one of the Catholic influences in the city, supervises the hospitals. In October 1864, Mobile's medical staff converted the Kennedy House Hotel in Mobile into the Heustis Hospital.[140] Additional medical facilities would be added before the end of the war.

Colonel Williams was still under court-martial and could not leave the city to visit his wife and son, now living in Prattville, Alabama. His extended stay exposed him to many men who had paid cash to the right person and were excluded from the Confederate army. He spoke harshly of the gentlemen who remained in the city but did not enlist in the Confederacy. He felt that the time would come when they would be ashamed that they had not served in the war.[141]

The secretary of war made his decision regarding Williams's situation: "In reply to your letter of Sept. 17th 1864 I am instructed by the Hon. Sec. of War to inform you that the Court having acquitted you there is no necessity or propriety in reviewing the record of court. Gen. Taylor, being your commanding officer, has the right to relieve you from command when in his discretion the good of the Service requires it."[142]

On October 22, conscription was expanded beyond what the Confederate government considered ideal soldiers for its army, and it also extended the call to the Creoles in the city: "An order appears in our paper this morning, requiring enrollment of the men of color in Mobile. The 'Creoles,' as they are proud to call themselves, have always been distinguished for their good order and well respect and since the commencement of the war have manifested their loyalty on all occasions, and we have no doubt they will, by the alacrity with which they respond to the order set a good example to all people of color in the city."[143]

Creoles, in Mobile, had the same rights at U.S. citizens. They were known at the "treaty population" since their freedom was granted as a part of the Louisiana Purchase in 1803 and the Adams-Oris Treaty in 1819. This tended to cause hostilities between Creoles and black Mobilians.[144] They were the only nonwhites in the state who could sell liquor, go to school and assemble with slaves. They represented one-third of the city's population of free people of color. They did not have much involvement in the slave community in Mobile.[145]

Previously, in 1862, General Dabney Maury, head of the Confederate Department of the Gulf, wrote to the secretary of war. He proposed enlisting Mobile Creoles. They did want to join the Confederacy and form their own unit. Yes, they were black, Maury acknowledged, but he reasoned that they did not stand on the same footing as other blacks. The secretary of war did not accept General Maury's request. If Mobile's Creoles could "naturally and properly" distinguish themselves from blacks, then they could wear the gray uniforms. The Creoles of Mobile clearly could not do this. They could only be employed as military laborers.[146] The desperate need for men to help defend the city seemed to suddenly ease the status of the Creoles in the city.

The Union siege of the city of Mobile was slowly beginning to work. The Confederate leaders in the city, the State of Alabama and other parts of this struggling rebellion were desperate for men to fight in its war. Winter was moving in, and the typical provisions were no longer available. The months ahead would reflect a drastic shift from Mobile's antebellum society to a new level of struggle and desperation for everyone.

Chapter 5

November 1864

Denial and Survival

*Should the base, plebeian rabble,
Dare assail me as I rant,
Seek my noble squaw, Octavia,
Weeping in her widowed home.
Seek her, say the guards have got me
Under their protecting wing,
Going to make me join the army,
Where the shell and Minnie sing.*[147]

There was a shift in the weather from warm and rainy to cool, clear and delightful.[148] The first signs of ice were seen in the city.[149] The majority of original Confederate States had not fallen to Union forces. Abraham Lincoln was reelected as president of the United States, and Andrew Johnson was elected as vice president.[150] On November 16, Confederate president Jefferson Davis called for a National Day of Prayer.[151]

The month of November emerged with four Union vessels spotted off the obstructions at Dog River bar, while action in the upper and lower Mobile Bay remained "remarkably quiet."[152] Major General Dabney Maury knew that these few months of stillness were only temporary. He continued his crusade to increase the number of soldiers to fight for the city.

If the Federals had known of, and responded to, the weakness of the Mobile stronghold, the city and what was left of the fracturing Confederacy could have fallen in a matters of days. Major General

Confederate president Jefferson Davis. *Courtesy of the Library of Congress.*

Maury briefed the Confederate governor of Alabama, Thomas H. Watts, of the situation:

I hope you will be able to raise and send to Mobile some state troops at a very early day. Four-thousand additional troops should be here as soon as possible and should be held here; otherwise this place may be carried by coup de main any night. I was repeatedly laid this fact before the proper authorities, but, as you'll understand, other paramount objects require the Confederate forces and the necessities of Mobile have been deferred to them. I receive such rumors of increasing force at Pensacola and in the lower bay as to compel me, since Hood's army has gone beyond reach, to see the last resort to avoid disaster.[153]

One dedicated soldier, recently released as part of a prisoner of war exchange,[154] could not be kept away from the action in Mobile. First Lieutenant Peter U. Murphey—or, as he was more popularly known, "Captain Pat"—of the steamer CSS *Selma* returned to the city weeks after his liberty from a Union prison. Perhaps he came to recover from his wounds or enjoy the still-festive atmosphere and to take advantage of his local popularity. "The captain looks good as new although still suffering from his wound. Although our naval commanders were compelled to lose the fight and their vessels, all of our people agree that our little navy did its whole duty and no tarnish rests upon its fair fame. Captain 'Pat' is gladly welcomed back by a large number of friends and people generally."[155]

The Mobile Theatre, located at the corner of Royal and Conti Streets,[156] helped those who still struggled to perpetuate the prewar way of life. The theater was the only remaining source of entertainment and amusement in the city.[157] However, theater productions in Mobile would have to rest for a short time in November. The train tracks for the Great Northern Railroad were damaged in a severe storm, and the theater corps riding the train from Montgomery, Alabama, did not arrive on time. It would be a week before another production could be held.[158] When the weather turned cold, the manager, in an effort to maintain attendance, went so far as to heat and warm the rooms so that the audience would not be cold.[159]

A gifted Jewish musician, Joseph Bloch played a seemingly unnoticeable but important role in many of the theater productions and other events held in Mobile during this time. While no actual documentation has been discovered to place him at specific balls or theater productions, his son wrote passionately about his father's role in Mobile during the Civil War—one of which was as concert-master of the Mobile Theatre Orchestra.[160]

Joseph Bloch. *Courtesy of the Springhill Avenue Temple Archives, Mobile, compiled by Susan Thomas.*

Joseph Bloch and his family, while not part of the highest social classes in the city, were able to survive the war by utilizing their talents and ingenuity. Born in a little village in Germany, Joseph immigrated to America in 1848. As he was traveling to New Orleans to find work, he came through Mobile. He met Miss Hannah Goldstucker, married her and decided to remain a part of the city for life.[161]

Joseph gave lessons to support his growing family. His ability to quickly learn new instruments earned him the position of concert-master of the local orchestra. In addition to working in the orchestra, Joseph also gave lessons to worthy individuals and taught at St. Joseph's Institute at Springhill for thirty-seven years.

> *He had the unique distinction of being the only non-Catholic ever to receive the Papal blessing which was conferred upon him by Pope Leo XVIII. It came about this way: the president of the college, having been*

received in audience by the Pope was taking his leave when His Holiness asked to have his blessing conveyed to the Fathers at Springhill College. The President said, "There is one amongst us, not of the Faith who has grown old in service to the College, and who is loved and honored by us all." His Holiness answered, "Then covey to him the blessing of one old man to another."[162]

Jews in the Confederate States served in all branches of the service and in all departments of the military, just like everyone else who qualified to serve; 105 served in the Alabama Infantry and 21 in the cavalry.[163] The Twelfth Alabama contained no fewer than 15 Jewish soldiers from Mobile.[164] Joseph Bloch's service as bugler with the Alabama State Artillery and enlistment with the Home Guard in Mobile was not unique. However, what did make him stand out was his passionate belief in a free government that could only be found in the Union.[165]

Edward Bloch recalled that his father was bitterly opposed to owning slaves but found himself in a challenging situation one Friday on his way to the market more than likely located on Mobile's Royal Street:

He was on his way to the public market one Friday morning to buy some fresh fish when he stopped at the Court house, the steps of which served as a slave market. The man called his attention to a mother and four children who had been brought down from the country to settle an estate and who were huddled together on the steps, weeping piteously at the prospect of lifelong separation. My Father, kind sympathetic soul that he was, was so overcome that he turned back, went at once to see his various relatives on behalf of the poor mother and before the day was over had arranged to have the entire family bought by them, so that they might continue to live near each other. Before that time my Mother had always hired slaves to help in the household, my Father always having refused to own another human being.[166]

Joseph Bloch, to protect his family, did not share his Unionist beliefs with the patrons who enjoyed his musical talents at the many events he must have been connected with in one way or another. To earn a living, he needed to play at numerous occasions, and his status in the Confederate army would make him an ideal candidate when it chose the musicians to play for fundraising balls held to help desperate soldiers in the field.

The night of November 25 was one such event. It would be among the best balls to be held in Mobile in quite some time. Held at the Odd Fellows

Hall in the Battle House on Royal Street, the ball was sponsored by the Young Men's Social Club with proceeds to go to the Continentals, Company A of the State Artillery:

> *A band of music discoursed various agreeable airs until 9 o'clock, when the dancing commenced—The number of ladies in attendance was very large.... The only regret expressed was the absence of the brave boys who were in the field, as all wished them here. The gentlemen composing the club have acted handsomely, and their efforts have doubtless met with a splendid reward, and the members of Company A will be the recipients of many comforts that they cannot receive with more pleasure than it was given by the club, blessed with the smiles of women.*[167]

Many of the citizens of Mobile who were living a comfortable lifestyle realized that costs of staples were rising. Even so, they were still amply supplied and did not feel the sting of the siege as did the less fortunate.[168] The affluent could buy corn and oats from W.H. Roberts and Company or wheat and poultry from H. Barkuloo & Company.[169] Anyone living in the city with a bit of garden space in their yard, and patience, could purchase a fresh supply of garden seeds from A.L. Pope.[170]

There was plenty of ostentatious and extravagant behavior by officials, but those of limited means were starting to experience difficulties as they struggled to obtain the basic necessities of life. Sara D. Eggleston of Mississippi recalled:

> *How any class of people except those who had gold to exchange for Confederate money could live under such a state of things is a mystery. It is not surprising that there were narrow escapes from bread riots more than once in Mobile, and doubtless other cities in the Confederacy. I witnessed a demonstration of the kind in Mobile. Dauphin Street, for several blocks, was thronged with poor women, mothers and wives of soldiers in the field, demanding food for themselves and children. I heard that finally the fire engines were ordered out, and the poor women dispersed at the point of the nozzle.*[171]

The city's underlying tension increased as the months passed with the Union threat so close. The Mayor's Court was where the cases of "drunk and down" or other crimes threatening the civility within the city was addressed. Robert H. Slough, Confederate mayor of Mobile, served as judge in many of the cases

Bread riots would happen many times in Mobile before Union occupation. "Southern Women Feeling the Effects of the Rebellion, and Creating Bread Riots." *Courtesy of the Library of Congress.*

brought to the downtown courtroom. Cases of all sorts came before the court. In one such case, a Mr. James T. Lyon was accused of murder:

> *The evidence went to show that Lyon was riding his horse on the sidewalk in front of Keenan's office or house, when Keenan came out and remonstrated*

with Lyon. During the remonstrance some harsh language was used. Lyon rode off, but came back and drew out his gun, threatening to shoot. Keenan dared him to do so, when Lyon raised his gun and fired, the ball taking effect in his left breast, and producing death in a very few minutes. Lyon was arrested by some cavalrymen, and delivered to Captain Dyson and committed to the guardhouse.[172]

While the Union fleet continued to reside in the bay within mere miles of Mobile, the time for Willie, the son of William Rix, to make his escape from Mobile and conscription in the Confederate army had arrived:

One Sunday morning, the last of the November, the north wind blew a gale, charged with the hyperborean chill of northern snowdrifts. It was one of those blasts that come a few times every winter over the genial Southern land to mock at the ides of absolute segregation from the north. At an early hour Capt. Merchant called to tell us that the schooner was waiting some three miles below, and that a carriage would be at the door, as soon as people were in church, to bear away our boy. Willie's mother was never so busy as during those two long hours of preparation and packing. The carriage came and we saw Willie, his great hazel eyes swimming in ill-suppressed tears disappeared behind drawn curtains and the negro driver whirl him from view.[173]

Unionists were not the only ones still trying to escape the city. Runaway slaves were still trying to reach the freedom offered by the Federal fleet: "Coroner Delshamps held another inquest near Catfish Point, on the body of a negro man clad in white pants and faded damesk shirt. Verdict: Found Drowned."[174] Was it better to lose so many slaves to Union forces to death by risking their lives reaching the Union fleet in the bay or to enlist those same slaves in the Confederate army? While the Confederate government had considered allowing slaves to fight in exchange for their freedom, the need suddenly became great, and many expressed their opinion on the matter: "But if we should make use of the negroes as soldiers, what would become of slavery?"[175]

Allowing slaves to fight for the Confederacy had long been a topic of heated discussion, and the city of Mobile was no different. By August 1863, Alabama's legislature had decided that since Union forces were enlisting and drafting slaves from the South, the Confederate states should at least counterbalance the force of insurgent blacks who stood against them. The topic of arming slaves was a constant feature in the *Mobile Advertiser and Register*, and the two parties debating did not give their actual names but rather debated under the titles of "Soldat" and "Citizen."[176] Would enlisting slaves to fight on behalf of the Confederacy save the struggling fight? The debate was to continue for months.

In November 1864, Jefferson Davis finally agreed to the principle of the idea. Although still denying that the Confederacy was in such a state that armed slaves would be its only hope, he did acknowledge that this could become an issue: "Davis asserted that in the future, if the situation were to worsen, and 'the alternate ever be presented of subjection of the employment of the slave as a solder, then one seems to doubt what should then be our decision.'"[177]

As the siege progressed, the struggle to maintain order grew. The affluent could still disguise their fear by enjoying the gaiety in the city, but how much longer could they pretend? As Mobile progressed into its winter season, the sting of the War of Separation would become sharp.

Chapter 6

DECEMBER 1864

The Call of Home

The bells hang silent in their towers,
Our country mourns her valiant dead;
E'en happy Childhood, trembling cowers,
Responsive to a nameless dread.
E'en Santa Claus must not be named,
His stores are scant, his servants scattered,
His sturdy limbs are hacked and marred,
His cheerful visage worn and battered.[178]

Lieutenant General Ulysses S. Grant wanted to move forward with the strike on Mobile, but Major General Edward R.S. Canby, commander of the Union Army of the Gulf, decided to settle in, build up forces and wait for the passage of winter season.[179] The weather continued to fluctuate but remained unusually warm, and some days were more like summer.[180]

Since the Battle of Mobile Bay, fewer and fewer Confederate blockade runners could slink past the Union ships guarding the ocean entrance to the bay. Cargo containing food and other supplies needed for the city to function had to come by rail or by steamers from northern places like Montgomery and Demopolis.[181] The city market remained tolerably well supplied, but prices were still high.[182] The prices for necessities would increase by the end of the month with the Union raid at Pollard, destruction of the train tracks and the fundraising efforts of the Christmas holidays.[183]

The Mobile Market and Mayor's Court House. "Old Market House, Mobile, Alabama." *Courtesy of the Library of Congress.*

In December 1864, Union forces stepped up their small raids along Mobile shores, and Confederate forces continued building up their navy and land defenses. Despite the growing crisis, Mobile's harbor was still producing ships for the Confederate navy. A new steamer was completed in Mobile, the *Rose Maury*, named after Major General Dabney Maury's daughter. Created as a mode of transportation between the city and its outer defenses, the ship would take its first trial run in Mobile Bay. Major Henry St. Paul was the designer of the steamer, and the layout was executed by William G. McKay of Mobile.[184] The low-pressure engine came from the workshops of Parks, Lyons and Keyland, better known for its assistance in developing the submarine the *Hunley*.[185]

Another practice in Mobile during this turbulent period in time was the municipal matters of the city and their functioning as they had in pre–Civil War days.[186] On December 5, 1864, with the Union fleet mere miles from the city, elections were held for the offices of mayor and councilmen, all for three-year terms:[187]

> *While the interest and excitement of the present canvas are admirable, perhaps greater than at any previous election since the war…it is monopolized by the offices which aforetime have caused no contention, and have almost gone "by default." For Mayor and Council there is but one ticket—the present Mayor and nearly all the present Council being candidates, without opposition, for re-election. That so important an office to the city as that of Mayor should be allowed to be filled without contest, argues general satisfaction with the present incumbent, or a remarkable scarcity of material wherewith to organize an opposition. Such a pacific and one-sided canvas for Mayor we have never before witnessed in Mobile. It certainly differs widely in this respect from that which resulted in the election of Mr. Slough.*[188]

Announcing the winners of the mayor and councilman elections may have not been necessary, since they ran uncontested, but the *Mobile Advertiser and Register* shared the results anyway. Mayor R.H. Slough would remain in office. In addition, Charles T. Ketchum would continue to represent the First Ward, D.P. Reid the Second Ward, George A. Ketchum the Third Ward, Daniel McNeill the Forth Ward, John King the Fifth Ward and John Hurtel the Sixth Ward; C.F. Moulton, who presided over the local court in Mayor Slough's stead, would represent the Seventh Ward.[189] The reelected mayor and councilmen were quickly sworn into office.[190]

The resolve of those in Mobile to be entertained in the blockaded city was amazing, and it seems that the Christmas holiday provided a reasonable justification for their efforts. The productions at the Mobile Theatre continued almost daily. If the spectacle did not entertain the men sufficiently, then they would form their own small parade to march through town. Finally, one had to remember that it was Christmas, and what better way to keep a mind off the current troubles then to help those gallant men and boys fighting for the Confederate cause. Fancy suppers and grand balls were arranged to raise funds to supply those soldiers with food and clothing.

Those in charge of the Mobile Theatre and its actors and actresses worked tirelessly to keep up the spirits and patronage of theatergoers in the city. December 11 saw cold weather begin to really set in, and management did all it could to keep its auditorium warm. It used two large stoves, fed with wood, and was making plans to add a third to keep its patrons happy.[191]

Mobile Theatre management persisted, despite the strain, in its efforts to create, or acquire, new material, even while trying to keep a city under siege entertained and distracted from what was happening. Productions began to be repeated, and probably from pure exhaustion, the actors and actresses could not maintain the quality of their performances as they had in the past:

> *We regret to be informed that the success of the company has not been commiserated with their efforts to please. The company is the largest that has been here for several seasons, embracing some of the best names in the Confederacy and they have labored hard to satisfy the public, and if they have not achieved success they have at least deserved it. The difficulties they had to encounter have been great, but the management are not discouraged, and are resolved to resort to additional expense and pains in the future. In addition to the great amount of novelty already furnished, we understand several new pieces are in preparation and will shortly be produced. Arrangements are also being made to render better light.*[192]

In a city known as the birthplace of Mardi Gras, it was not strange for the men in town to travel through the streets and celebrate. On December 4, a number of naval officers stationed in Mobile wanted to make Captain Murphy of the CSS *Selma* feel welcome. He had recently returned to the city and was still recovering at the home of Captain George W. Harrison of the CSS *Morgan*. These officers formed a parade of their own and traveled to the Harrison household.

When "Captain Pat" came out of the house, the men were singing around the front porch. At the choir's conclusion, a speech was given, and Captain Murphy answered in kind: "Captain Murphy responded in his usual, happy and natural style, his arm, which he still carries in a sling, giving to his remarks a greater effect than the most appropriate gestures should produce, speaking so eloquently as it did of the desperate fight of the 5th of August, when all was lost save honor, while that accrued solely to the vanquished party in the unequal contest."[193]

Captain Pat Murphy was not the only man to be welcomed home in this fashion in December 1864. Admiral Raphael Semmes, captain of the commerce raider CSS *Alabama*, had survived the sinking of his ship and, after traveling across the diminishing Confederate territory, made it to his family home in Mobile.[194]

Admiral Raphael Semmes, after serving in the Mexican-American War, chose to live in Mobile, which he considered home for the remainder of his life.[195] When the state of Alabama succeeded from the United States, Semmes decided to align his loyalties with the Confederacy. He spent two years traveling the Atlantic and Indian Oceans, evading Union ships

Surviving the Union Blockade

Right: Admiral Raphael Semmes. "Captain Semmes, of the Pirate *Alabama*." Courtesy of the Library of Congress.

Below: Sinking of the CSS *Alabama*. "Last of the Alabama Commodore Winslows Grand Victory March. Respectfully Inscribed to the Crew of the *Kearsarge*." Courtesy of the Library of Congress.

or capturing vessels for the Confederate fleet.[196] In June 1864, Semmes's success evading Union forces would come to an end with the sinking of the CSS *Alabama*. He decided to return home to Mobile, Alabama, to be with his family.

The journey home began in October 1864 aboard the steamer *Tasmanian*, headed for Havana, Cuba. His plan was to enter the Confederacy through Texas, since the blockade at Mobile and the surrounding area was considerable. Semmes commented on the Union plans, "The enemy having to resort, literally, to the starving process, as being the only one that was likely to put an end to the war, had begun to burn our towns, lay waste our corn fields, run off our negroes and cattle, and was now endeavoring to seal, hermetically, our ports."[197]

He traveled by ship and carriage to the town of Matamoras, Mexico. He then met with Colonel John Salmon Ford, the commandant at Brownsville, Texas. They snuck across the Rio Grande in the middle of the night, and Semmes rejoiced over returning to his native South. He continued across the state of Texas by coach, reaching Shreveport, Louisiana, by November 27. Semmes's next mode of transportation was by carriage and horseback, across the Red and Mississippi Rivers, having to evade Union forces along the way. After months of travel, he finally made it to his home in Mobile.[198]

The news that Admiral Raphael Semmes had returned to the city spread quickly. Only a few days after his return home, another serenade was commenced by the men. This group was led by the First Louisiana Band, which marched to his residence at the northwest corner of Government and Wilkins Streets:

> *The valiant Commander appeared and spoke for about ten minutes....He said that we ought to be thankful that this war had occurred in our generation, that the eyes of all Europe were admiring the heroism with which our forces, on land and sea, were battling for our right and liberties and that we should live after ages on the pages of a history such as the world has never before produced. He concluded by thanking once more his fellow townsmen of Mobile for the pleasing and delicate complement after which three cheers, three times for Capt. Semmes and three for the Alabama, were proposed. Three cheers echoed from the crowd.*[199]

In addition to events such as the theater and street serenades, the wealthy people of Mobile busied themselves with what they called suppers and grand balls. These events now served a dual purpose. They would be an opportunity to celebrate and bring a bit of joy to the current situation and would also become fundraisers to help Confederate soldiers in the field or those in Union prisons, like Ship Island.

Ship Island, so very close to Mobile and containing many Confederate soldiers from Mobile and Alabama, became the focus of flag-of-truce boats carrying vegetables and other useful articles.[200] Helping those soldiers and others in need became the focus of charity efforts during the Christmas holidays.[201] When those in Mobile learned of the terrible conditions of the Confederate prisoners at Ship Island, they were quick to use any means to improve their quality of life, including the sending of Duff C. Green, brigadier general and quartermaster general of Alabama, to see the situation for himself, and the selling of two hundred bales of cotton in New Orleans to provide food, clothing and necessary comforts.[202]

One such event was a supper held by the Soldiers' Friend Society at the Odd Fellows Hall in the Battle House hotel:

> *Christmas, the season for festivity, is at hand, and the opening feat of the season comes off to-night at Odd Fellows Hall. It is most righteously dedicated to our soldiers in the field and in captivity, and let us hope that, thus sanctified, the enjoyments of this close of the year will meet with the approving smiles of Heaven. With this seeming in their hearts, let all present themselves with their offering. Arrangements have been made for a splendid supper, worthy of the cause for which it is given.*[203]

Lieutenant Colonel Williams remained in the city and was put in charge of the Appalachee Batteries located about fifteen miles south of the city. He was eager to travel north to see his wife and son but quickly learned that chances for that were remote: "I feel that I will certainly be disappointed in my hopes of meeting you Christmas as the enemy appear to be threatening the city— The town is full of rumors and until these quiet down I could not succeed in obtaining leave of absence from so important a command. I will watch the indications and as soon as there is a ghost of a chance for success."[204]

On December 20, less than a week before Christmas, the *Mobile Advertiser and Register* announced the battle at Pollard, Alabama. Pollard, a major railroad depot, was less than one hundred miles from Mobile. The Pollard raiders attacked on the eighteenth but were driven back by the forces on Mobile's Eastern Shore. The town of Pollard did suffer from the Union raid. The raiders managed to damage the railroad tracks of the Mobile & Great Northern Railroad, and the public buildings in Pollard were burned.[205]

The weather gradually turned colder, and the need for wood, for heating and cooking, became greater. The city continued to provide wood to those who could not afford the inflated prices. The change in weather caused the people of Mobile to begin to experience wood shortages.[206] A committee formed to help provide wood to the poor in the city was able to have a load delivered to Mobile by boat at the foot of St. Michael Street.[207]

When Christmas came to Mobile, some managed to make the best of the situation, whereas others could see nothing but the end coming. Kate Cummings recalled, "What vision of cheer does not the sound of 'Merry Christmas' bring in review—happiness, plenty and a forgetting, for a few short hours, the care of this weary world. This one has been anything but merry to us. A gloom has hung over us all, and that do what we will we cannot dispel. Our thoughts involuntarily wander to where our brave armies are struggling against fearful odds. Alas! When, will this strife and bloodshed cease? When shall we have peace?"[208]

Union forces of about one thousand men began building up at Franklin Mills on Dog River, just south of the city. The location was a difficult one, very swampy, and the only way they could get supplies was by traveling Dog River itself. Confederate soldiers and native Mobilians who knew the land guarded the position to make sure that the Yankee forces would not move farther north.[209] Heavy musketry and artillery fire were heard from the direction of Goode's Mill from Confederate forces below the city.[210] The relative quiet that had been the norm in the city was beginning to be replaced with the renewed echoes of gunfire.

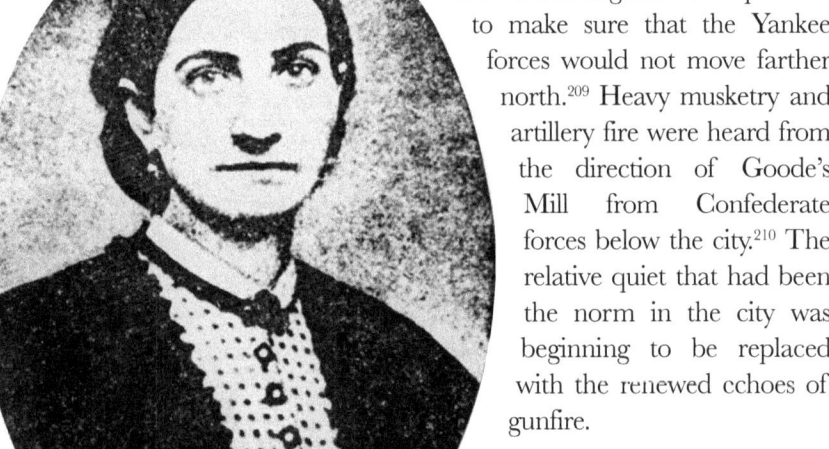

Kate Cummings. *Courtesy of the Delaney Collection, History Museum of Mobile, compiled by Nick Beeson.*

Miss Cummings summed up the end of the year of 1864 with these tragic words:

> *December 31ˢᵗ: The last day of 1864, and much coveted peace seemingly as distant as ever. Were it not for the knowledge that there is an end to all things, and that someday there will be an end to this, it would be unbearable. The past year has equaled any of its predecessors for carnage and bloodshed. Our land is drenched with the blood of martyrs. Her fair hills and valleys are lit by blazing homesteads, and echo to the booming of artillery and the roar of musketry; the very air is rent with the groans of the wounded and dying, and the wail of the widow and orphan. Lord, turn not thy face from us; and save us, O, save us from this terrible scourge! Let not our sins now cry against us for vengeance!*[211]

Chapter 7

JANUARY 1865

Settle the Contradictions

*O Father! Interpose thy aid
And stop this cruel strife,
Does Justice unappeased still call
For sacrifice of life!
The bravest of our Southern sons
Sleep low beneath the sod
How saddened hearts now grieve for them
None knows, but Thou, oh God!*[212]

At this point, $100 in Union gold equaled $3,400 in Confederate money.[213] Five hundred gallons of Catawba wine could be purchased on consignment.[214] Metal could be traded in for a variety of goods, including gunpowder and corn.[215] Union blockaders continued to roll with the waves in Mobile Bay, anchored off the Dog River bar.[216] Federal forces were steadily increasing in Union-held Pensacola and Fort Gaines.[217]

The Southern War for Independence was now in its fifth year,[218] but there was a broadening fear that it would not reach its sixth or even the summer. Mobile received word that Union general William T. Sherman had taken Savannah, Georgia. Confederate general John Bell Hood was defeated at the Battle of Nashville. Those loyal to the Confederacy started the year full of gloom and despondency.[219] Yet, in exercising true Southern hospitality, they made the best of the situation and provided for the rebel soldiers guarding the forts and batteries.

Confederate general John Bell Hood. *Courtesy of the Library of Congress.*

Battery Tracy received unexpected rations from the embattled city: "Our hearts throb with gratitude to those kind friends in Mobile, who have remembered us in our isolated position. Grim visage war was today forgotten, as we gave ourselves up to feasting and thanksgiving….It would have done your soul good to have seen us in convention around our camp tables, discussing the merits of each dish as the vast turkey, beef, mutton, and pork, potatoes and hot biscuits, were rapidly transferred from pan to plate and from plate—to that borne from which no turkey ever returns."[220]

Shortages were gradually becoming more common, but certain foods continued to be large in surplus: "Local livestock, especially hogs, were plentiful in Mobile, and meat supplies regularly came to the Alabama port from the state's interior and sold meat for relatively reasonable prices."[221]

The city was increasingly showing small signs of suffering under the Union blockade. Winter was coming to its coldest time of year, and the typical lifeless hues of the season were magnified by the conditions of the blockade. Kate Cummings, a Mobile resident and Confederate nurse, wrote of the military presence in the city and the determination not to surrender. She also told of how the once beautiful gardens in the city were now destroyed: "The fine shade trees, beautiful shrubbery and lovely flower gardens once the boast of Mobile, were laid waste by the military authorities for fear of giving shelter to the enemy. It was a sad sight to visit the suburbs and see the desolation, but anything was better than having the Yankees among us. Immense entrenchments were dug all around the city."[222]

While the Confederate losses were felt in all parts of the South, there was a bit of good news for those in Mobile in early January: Confederate soldiers captured at Fort Gaines during the Battle of Mobile Bay arrived home after being exchanged for Union prisoners. The negotiations for the release of these soldiers was intense and began as early as September 1864, but after the details of the exchange were worked out, more than six hundred soldiers, many of them Mobile natives, were coming home.[223]

Large numbers of people flocked to the wharves to welcome the ships carrying these men and hear of their experiences in captivity.[224] The Confederate Exchange Bureau worked out accommodations for relatives and friends and took care of soldiers who were not from Mobile by providing good quarters and rations:[225] "Their sufferings had been the direct consequence of their position on one of the outposts of Mobile defenses, and the obligations the people of the city and of the State are not the less their due.…Something more is due them than a military escort, with bands of music and a crowd of people to meet them."[226]

Lieutenant Colonel James M. Williams was placed in charge of the exchanged prisoners, but they were furloughed for fifteen to twenty days after their release.[227] He was still reeling from the Fort Powell affair. His name had been cleared officially, but the *Mobile Advertiser and Register* and its editor, John Forsyth, had not retracted the negative statements that were made.

A letter to his wife, Lizzy, shows that a retraction was finally printed: "I enclose you a scrap from the *(Mobile) Advertiser & Register* of the 31st—You will see that Mr. Forsyth has at last set himself right towards me—and (this is a secret you must keep) I'll tell you what opened his eyes—I challenged him—or rather sent him such a letter as usually precedes a challenge. He said that he must apologize or fight and so—this article—I accepted it and now that it's over and I am no longer in danger of being killed in a duel, I tell you of it."[228]

William Rix could also breathe a sigh of relief, for he had heard from his son, Willie, and the amazing adventure he experienced, in the letter he sent to his mother. When the blockade runner carrying Willie tried to sneak past the Union-occupied forts at the mouth of Mobile Bay, Fort Morgan spotted the boat and fired a shot that woke up the entire Union fleet:

> *I was in the stern of the ship when, very suddenly I saw a streak of lightning, but did not think any more about it. I had just got seated, when, whiz-z-z, boom—you ought to have seen me tumble into the cabin, between the cotton bales. I got down there quicker than ever a prairie-dog tumbled into its hole. I expected every moment to see cotton bales, cannon balls, and the whole side of the ship come into the cabin. I kept below about fifteen minutes, and thought then the danger was over and I would go on deck to see the fun of passing the fleet. I had hardly got my head out of the cabin when very unpleasant sounds struck my ears—whiz-z—bang—boom—whiz-z—boom—the shells were screaming all around us. One of them exploded very near the bow of the ship. Such a romantic sight I never witnessed before in my life—balls whizzing, shells exploding—every ship in the fleet lighted up. Well, my dear mother, we were captured, but it was not the shells that "brought us to." We kept on till the steamer Kansas ran alongside of us; when we struck our colors! We were taken on board the steamer and carried down a hole, where we were stripped naked and everything we had taken from us—not even a tooth pick was left in my pocket…I remained on the flagship almost a week, and was treated kindly. Commodore Thatcher took me under his care. He let me take his glass up aloft to look toward home; but I could not see any of you. I arrived in New Orleans on the 6th and have been here two weeks as a paroled prisoner.*[229]

While William Rix, a Unionist still living in the city, was able to help his son escape conscription into the Confederate army, those who still lived in Mobile managed to avoid military service or they were absent without authorization. "The people of Mobile are failing in their duties," wailed the *Register*, which complained that there were plenty of men to fill the army among the speculators who "should be as eager to fly to the front as they are now to respond to the cajoling of the auctioneer." The newspaper also blasted the leaders of the community. "Why are they not calling 'come on boys fight by our side,'" it asked? "All these men are men of influence in the community, and if they would shoulder their muskets, their example would be followed by the hundreds." But such rebukes fell on deaf ears, as most Mobilians, by early 1865, were reluctant participants in a war and a cause that they considered long since lost.[230]

Despondency was quickly becoming a true danger to the Confederates who naïvely thought that their fledgling nation and slavery could continue. After fighting for four years and not appearing any closer to victory, many were ready to embrace almost any terms the United States would offer to put an end to the war. The *Mobile Advertiser and Register* was full of hopeful and promising words during this trying time, dedicated to lifting spirits, but to little effect.[231]

These feelings of hopelessness on the part of the Confederate soldiers and people who remained in the city could easily be expected. They knew that the Union army was slowly working its way toward Mobile and realized that they might see death before the war ending. While some disheartened men decided to run from the Confederate army, others sought to escape the situation in other ways.

Mobile, a city known for parties and a fair amount of drinking, could not get the good wine and whiskey imported from Havana and other far-off places. Instead, the blockade led to the creation of the vilest of drinks to be concocted and sold under the names of "whiskey" and "rum." Constructed of native plants such as sorghum, pine knots and china berries, the "whiskey" sold for fifty to seventy-five dollars per quart. "Drinking grew to be a common vice, and did great harm to the cause."[232]

The Customhouse, located at the heart of Mobile on Royal Street, was the location of the principal Confederate government and civil government. The inhabitants complained that the Customhouse was surrounded by drinking houses and that officers visited them too frequently. They complained of the large drinking house exactly opposite the Customhouse, more than likely the Battle House, and of at least two others along St. Francis Street. "In a military point of view, is not the situation rather critical? The enemy is in heavy force in front and on both flanks....Poor Confederate citadel! Besieged by drinking shops! An officer can't enter into it or leave it without being exposed to the enemy's fire."[233]

As the month of January 1865 progressed, the conditions in the city became unfavorable. On January 10, a hailstorm blew in, tearing up trees and shrubs and probably endangering the small crops that gardeners were trying to grow for the local street markets.[234] Marketers shared the grim news that there would be fewer vegetables available: "They say it is useless to attempt

The Battle House, Mobile, Alabama. *Courtesy of the Library of Congress.*

to raise vegetables…for the straggling soldiers will allow nothing green to sprout out the ground without pouncing upon it. If this general pilfering is not stopped neither soldiers nor citizens will be able to eat vegetables the coming season, and a vegetable famine awaits us."[235]

The "strike of the match" moment that triggered the true change of conditions in Mobile seems to be the knowledge of how dramatically General Hood lost in Tennessee and the panic that resulted in the gold market.[236] The Confederate army was demoralized by the defeat and losses at Tennessee. Kate Cummings's brother, a participant in the battle at Franklin, relayed to her the conditions: "The sufferings of our men on the retreat seemed to have reached a climax, for all they had heretofore undergone was nothing in comparison. Many of them were shoeless, and left their blood on the snow, the flesh actually dropping from their feet. My brother saw a man, after they arrived in Tupelo, having both feet amputated from being frozen, and no doubt there were many others like him."[237]

The accelerated changes in currency value affect everyone. Previously, the blockade had affected only the families of soldiers or those who provided

Confederate dollar bill issued in Mobile, Alabama. *Courtesy of the Delaney Collection, History Museum of Mobile, compiled by Nick Beeson.*

services to those who had not yet felt the pinch of war. Now, even the wealthy citizens of Mobile began to do without. The value of gold went up but then dropped back down suddenly. The uncertain prices caused the luxury items taken for granted only days and weeks before to increase. There was a huge advance in the cost of sugar and coffee, if they were available. "Those who wish for 'sweet things' have to 'pay for the whistle.'"[238]

When the month concluded, there was a dramatic rise in the cost of provisions, groceries and breadstuffs. The cost of flour increased from $300 per barrel to $400 per barrel.[239] Some began to feel as if vendors were exhorting the last dollar from every man, without any moral obligation. "We did not extend our inquiry further, being apprehensive if we did so our faith in the honesty of our fellows, already somewhat weakened since the war, might be still further lessened."[240]

Distrust extended beyond the vendors making a living in Mobile and would bleed down to slaves and free blacks trying to survive the war as well. The mayor, in his court, toughened laws and inflicted harsh punishments for men of color. "Such ordinances were established during the antebellum period but were not always rigorously enforced. During the war, however, they were strictly enforced, and in some cases even more strictly, as the conflict drew to a close and white fears of slave uprising intensified."[241]

Tension increased in Mobile between the different races, and the status of those who were trying to survive to see the end of this very uncivil war was debated heavily. The rhetoric in the *Mobile Advertiser and Register* continued to examine the issue of allowing the slaves to fight on behalf of the Confederacy and provide the desperately needed manpower. The contention continued at the Confederate House of Representatives on allowing the enlistment of blacks; finally, it passed a bill for their employment in the army.[242]

A Confederate soldier, an officer of rank, fighting for Mobile at Fort Blakeley, located directly across Mobile Bay on the Eastern Shore, sent a powerful letter to the *Advertiser and Register* and explained the situation in a way that many could not deny. He suggested the Confederate government decide to set all slaves free and not only those who would fight on behalf of the Confederacy:

> *Your position…for the incorporation of negroes in our armies, is an inexorable necessity, and will be readily admitted by any reflecting man, who loves his country better than himself. But it, alone, is not sufficient to accomplish the work for independence.…Is there no such thing as being too late in applying remedies for evil? Then, I ask, will not emancipation, made gradual to suit the necessities of the times, neutralize at one blow the moral effect of Lincoln's proclamation, abroad and at home? Will it not convince the world that we are in earnest to obtain our independence, and draw from the Yankee its moral and physical support? Then will be settled the contradiction of a people fighting for freedom and slavery at the same time and in its stand will arise the question—Why does the Yankee continue to contest? The south has yielded slavery, and struck from the abolitionist his only hope of subjugation.*[243]

The Confederate government still had a hold on the city, but for how much longer? The newly christened ironclad *Rose Maury* caught fire and sank to the bottom of Mobile Bay, a total loss. When the fire reached the magazine, containing a number of shells, the people in the city were startled by the ensuing explosion, giving rise to fears and rumors.[244] There was one small exchange between the Confederate and Union fleets before the month was out. "In the Upper Bay, yesterday, there was a goodly number of discharge from heavy guns, which at one time was supposed to be an attack on one of our batteries by a monitor. The whole affair was a little target practice on our part, and the discharge of quite a number of guns from one of the enemy's vessels. About 1 o'clock she moved down the Bay."[245]

The weather began to turn extremely cold for the city located in the Deep South, and there was another threat of snow.[246] It was becoming clear that

Magnolia Cemetery, Mobile, Alabama. *Courtesy of the Library of Congress.*

everyone was tired of this war and just wanted to see the struggle end. They were tired of losing loved ones—husbands, fathers and sons. The people still trying to survive in Mobile were finally tired of burying the dead.

Magnolia Cemetery, located on the western outskirts of Mobile, is the resting place for more than one thousand Confederate dead.[247] Those who had fought and met their final ends for the Confederate States of America deserved a decent, Christian burial. This did not happen for one deceased soldier. His body was left in a plain box, unburied, in the new graveyard. His coffin sat on the ground for days. The forgotten soldier was reported to the *Mobile Advertiser and Register*, which commented, "Such neglect, to call it by no harsher words, deserves prompt inquiry and severe rebuke."[248]

Chapter 8

February 1865

Speculations and Spies

*Nothing to drink, I can't get a drop,
For the Gov'nor has closed every rum shop
It rains every day; don't you think that he ought
Give us some whiskey to mix with the water?
Now was I an officer with bars on, I think
At a club room could get plenty to drink!
But I'm only a private, and is "drunk and down"
I'll have to pay an X for the good of the town.
An officer, forsooth, can cut up his capers
And not have his name appear in the papers.*[249]

President Abraham Lincoln met with Confederate peace officers at Fortress Monroe[250] at Hampton, Virginia, to try and reach an agreement, but there would be no peace unless the Confederate states returned to the Union.[251] Slaves were still being sold on the Mobile Courthouse steps to settle debts.[252] Steamers would leave Mobile for Pickensville and Demopolis.[253] "Indian Pain Killer," a possible substitute for liquor, could be purchased at L.C. Dubois and Company.[254] Firewood sold for twenty dollars per load.[255] At the port, steamers brought to the city potatoes, corn, beeswax, salt molasses, peas, oats, whiskey, lime, coal and cotton bales.[256]

The Union blockade of Mobile Bay did not completely stop groceries and supplies from reaching the city by the Mobile River, but it did change a standard in everyday life: coffee. The blockade runner *Gray Jacket* had earned

Festorazzi Coffee Saloon in Mobile, Alabama. *Courtesy of the Delaney Collection, History Museum of Mobile, compiled by Nick Beeson.*

enormous sums of money during the Civil War by running cotton to Havana, Cuba. It would sell the cotton to the English government in exchange for sugar, tobacco, rum, coffee and tea. After the taking of the forts, these items became scarce articles in Mobile.[257] It was surprising to see how the scarcity of coffee affected how everyone felt. There were people who, before the war, did not seem to care for it, but during the war it seemed to affect their mood greatly.[258] Extreme measures were made to develop substitutes for this drink. Citizens created a variety of mixtures using grains, okra seed, rice, peanuts, cotton seed, English peas, beans and sweet potatoes.[259] One lady remarked, "We ceased to make odd faces over it at last, even when sweetened with molasses and taken without milk."[260]

A popular recipe for a coffee substitute made it into the *Mobile Advertiser and Register* early in February 1865. Devised by a Mrs. Robert Holt, she served it to the people staying at her home, which doubled as a boardinghouse. They enjoyed the mixture so much that she was asked to share it with everyone:

Take three parts of well dried sweet potato, one part okra seed, parch them separately with care and grind them separately. Then mix thoroughly, and keep in a closely stopped vessel. Take one pound of sugar and put it into a pan or skillet, set it on the fire, constantly stirring until it is burnt to a dark brown, then pour on it half a gallon of boiling water, stirring it all the time till the whole is dissolved into thin syrup, put it into bottles and cork it. To make the coffee for five or six persons, take a half of a pint of the ground mixture, three tablespoonful's of the syrup, and put them into a bowl and stir into it a half a pint of water, let it stand fifteen minutes, and then put into the coffee pot and pour the boiling water to it, set it on the coals or stove five or ten minutes and then set it by to cool, then pour it into the urn, and serve it with boiled milk or cream.

Despite the growing scarcity of essentials in Mobile, the party-like atmosphere continued as best it could. The ladies, the gentlemen who continued to escape conscription and the soldiers who could get into town took every opportunity to gather despite their current conditions. A ball was held at the end of January at Temperance Hall off St. Joseph's Street, where Mardi Gras kings and queens were usually crowned.[261] Given by the Fidelis Society for the benefit of orphans who lost their families in the war, the ball was reportedly a success.[262] Another well-known event was the Creole Fair, held in benefit of the soldiers: "When festivity meant only festivity, the Mobile Creoles were never behindhand, and from the time that it has also involved acts of beneficence they have shown an equal forwardness with any class of our people to aid in the good cause. Their old friends will be sure to remember them on this occasion, and strangers will find the fair well worthy of a visit."[263] Confederate soldiers were also invited to parties at homes of wealthy citizens in Mobile. William Taylor Mumford, of the First Louisiana Heavy Artillery Regiment, found himself invited to Mrs. Raphael Semmes's house one fateful evening and spent a pleasant time dancing with the ladies until two o'clock on the morning.[264]

On February 3, the complaints of citizens the previous month and the threat of Union troops organizing in Pensacola resulted in a very dramatic move on behalf of the governor of Alabama to issue a proclamation, specifically for Mobile, to close all barrooms in the city, effective immediately.[265] Mayor Slough relayed the order the next day: "The Governor, under an act of legislature, approval November 17, 1863, having suspended the retailing of Spirituous Liquors in the city of Mobile, it is hereby ordered that all Barrooms and Drinking Saloons be closed—that all parties, in any manner violating the said law by retailing, will be dealt with as the law directs."[266]

The order to close bars and drinking saloons in Mobile was not a new one, but this time it would be strictly enforced. Just days after the mayor issued the order, a woman was accused of selling liquor without a license and fined fifty dollars or thirty days in city jail.[267] The closing of all drinking facilities in the city would be an issue of intense debate. One perspective saw it as a necessity. The officers and soldiers were getting so intoxicated that they would have trouble protecting the city from Union forces. It wasn't like other methods of managing the situation had not been tried, and to arrest and punish just the offenders would require so many city guards that it could equal that of the army. The other perspective saw it as unjust to those who paid good money for their business licenses, borrowed money and had other expenses that came from running a business. It wasn't their fault that the soldiers got drunk. Many felt that while soldiers were no longer able to get liquor, officers were certainly still able to get access to it. It was obvious that everyone was not of one mind on this issue: "One thing, however, is certain, the evil of drunkenness among army officers is a great one, and should be arrested in some way, and it is equally certain that any officer guilty of the crime, (for it is a crime in view of the circumstances) is unfit to exercise command."[268]

In addition to unrest between the soldiers, there was a clear divide between the longtime citizens who did not see the need for freeing slaves in exchange for fighting and those who did. One man, informing everyone that he was sixty-three years old, commented:

> *I am at a loss to understand why these two subjects are continually connected, or rather united, making one the inevitable consequence of the other. There is no connection or relationship between them; none whatever, and sir, there is no condition or circumstance growing out of the employment of our young negro men as soldiers, to the extent that we can safely go, with a proper regard to the cultivation of the soil plentifully, say eighty or one hundred thousand, that can or will, in the future, our independence gained, necessarily lead to emancipation beyond themselves.*[269]

The second week of February found increased speculations of an upcoming attack on Mobile. Everyone who remained in the interior of Alabama and Mississippi understood how important it was for Mobile to not allow Union forces past the bay. They strongly felt that the city itself was well protected—about anything outside the city limits they were not so sure.[270] All eyes were on General William T. Sherman and where he would march his men next.

What is significant is that they were paying attention to the makeup of his army. It was reported that his forty thousand Union troops were composed largely of black men. What would happen if the Confederate army had such a number? Many Southern sympathizers were caving to the comparison:

> *Suppose we had 25,000 black soldiers, drilled and officered by the veterans of the army, to add to our strength in Sherman's front!... Sherman would be out numbered, foiled, beaten, in what he destined the master military movement of the war....We beg the earnest attention of Gov. Watts to these facts. He already hears the din of warlike preparation in the northern part of the State; of Yankee soldiers mounting in heavy columns to sweep through the State. If Gov. Watts will take this initiative and the responsibility, he can shield the commonwealth from the threatened avalanche. Let him empower ten tried and experienced field officers to raise ten brigades of negroes for State defenses.*[271]

William T. Sherman. *Courtesy of the Library of Congress.*

On February 12, 1865, a very special letter appeared at the office of the *Mobile Advertiser and Register*. When the letter was published, it simply contained "A Woman's Thoughts" and did not designate any particular lady as its author, but it could have been one of the many prominent women in Mobile at the time. She would not have been afraid to communicate her thoughts to the editor, John Forsyth.

This letter was significant. With Sherman's forces fighting their way toward Mobile and Union general Canby building up forces to attack the city in Pensacola, this Confederate woman commented:

The dread which Southerners have of laying hands spun the Ark of a hastily-framed Constitution, is killing us. The Confederacy is perishing like the king of Spain who was burned to death because it was treason for a subject to lay hands upon the royal person. I would rather see a Dictator, than know that we are falling to pieces because no hand has the power to prop the crumbling ruin of our nationality. The time for talking about arming the slaves has gone by—it is easy to see that it has found favor with the people and today we must act....If the spirit is once aroused cannot the power to accept these slaves be vented somewhere, so that when the Rip Van Winkles who snore at Richmond shall awake, the forces may be ready to come at their call?...I do believe there is gold and silver enough in the hands of the women to redeem the currency of this country. Let us try at least if the women of Alabama will not do like the women of Russia? If the offering prove fruitless, it will be easy to return to each one what she has sent. I am ready to offer mine. It is worth...about $1000. It has all the value of association, but I would not keep it an hour if it could help the sick currency of the country....Many a woman who would deny her service of silver to a written appeal, would yield it to an electric touch of adroit eloquence. Just think of it, that there should be silver and gold and jewels enough in the country to redeem the currency!—I have just heard of Lincoln's reply to our Commissioners. Short of peace, it is exactly what we could most desire. It will prove to the reconstructionist that the most they have to hope for in the Union is a silken rope or the worthless book of a dishonored life.[272]

The call for each woman to do what she could, especially raise $1,000 each, was a bold one. The loyal Confederate citizens of Mobile tried to build up its people yet again. This time they formed the Society of Loyal Confederates.[273] They rallied at the Mobile Theatre and passed a resolution to call on the government to put 100,000 slaves into the Confederate army immediately.[274] Their voices seem to have been heard because about the same time as this meeting, Confederate president Davis assigned Brigadier General John T. Morgan with the task of organizing one-fourth of the male slave population for military use: "It was provided that recruiting officers were to establish stations wherever they deemed it necessary and that recruits were to report by May 1, 1865. Furthermore, all commissioned officers were authorized to enlist slaves. No enlistments were made without the consent of the owners, and the title of the slaves would not be affected."[275]

Surviving the Union Blockade

Battle of Franklin. *Courtesy of the Library of Congress.*

Confederate soldiers were being channeled toward Mobile to build up its forces, but they arrived in desperate condition. When the men in Holtzclaw's Alabama Brigade and a part of the Army of Tennessee made it to Mobile, it became obvious just how badly the men had suffered in the Battle of Franklin and others in Tennessee. The Confederate government could not supply them with shoes and clothing. Many of them arrived in Mobile barefoot and in rags. They had not received any sort of payment since April of the previous year, and they were in desperate need. An appeal was made for the people of Mobile to help purchase clothes and shoes for them. A blockade runner full of such supplies had recently made it past the Union fleet, and the money was to go toward this purchase. They must have received the necessary funds because Kate Cummings remarked in her journal, "The people revived after the Tennessee disaster, and all tried to make it as pleasant as possible for the survivors. I attended several of the parties at which our troops wore their old gray uniforms. If any appeared in citizen's dress it was because they had lost their clothes in the retreat. A large steamer ran the blockade about this time laden with clothes, and we scarcely recognized our boys in their fine new uniforms."[276]

The struggle to build up the number of Confederate troops by suggesting that slaves be allowed to fight and by sending more soldiers to the city was not enough. Not only was Mobile surrounded by Union forces building up their armies and waiting out the cold weather and the rain, but it was also subjected to spying. One spy, a man by the name of Perry Ryales, was a shoemaker and was acting on behalf of Union forces.

Due to the scarcity and cost of shoes in Mobile, his position allowed him access to information unlike any other. He was able to get a detailed account of the number of men, of the guns, the batteries, the obstructions, the boats in the bay and the weaknesses in the city.[277] Ryales escaped to Union forces and shared his valuable information.[278] Another group of "Galvanized Yankees"[279] was preparing to desert to the Union about this same time and take with it drawings and plans of the defenses of Mobile. Major General Dabney Maury organized a sting operation and captured the traitors before they could escape.[280]

As the month of February progressed, the quiet that everyone had experienced for months prior was gradually coming to an end. Union forces began to move, and Mobile was their objective. The threat of battle was increasing daily:[281]

> *This is a subject that interests Alabama and Mississippi as well as this city, for it is not the capture of Mobile only, but the conquest of those two States, that is designated. We have already said that Mobile cannot be carried by assault by land or by water. Our works are the most formidable character, our ordnance heavy and abundant, and our garrison is composed of the choicest veterans of the Confederate army. But no city situated like this, though it cannot be stormed, is exempt from the danger of a protracted siege and a long and complete investment. However ample the stores, if the investment is maintained, time will consume them. The lesson we would impress upon the people of the interior of the two States to which Mobile is the gateway, is that we can hold the city and do our part amply long enough to enable them to do what is necessary for their safety.*[282]

The struggle to keep up morale and the belief that the Confederacy could continue would lessen by the end of February. Laura Roberts Pillians wrote in her journal:

> *A day of intolerable gloom. Rain has been falling steadily for a week and as if in accordance with the weather comes the most dismal tidings*

from South Carolina. Charleston, the brave old city, the cradle wherein was nursed our sublime creed of government, has been evacuated by our government forces, is now garrisoned by negro soldiers, and old Fort Sumter that had bade defiance to the foe for days is now in the hands of the insolent enemy. Columbia has been burned and hundreds of women and children are homeless and starving. When will our woes cease?[283]

The last day of February saw Union movement after months of quiet and inactivity. Twenty-eight enemy vessels, including six Mississippi transports, were spotted by rebel scouts off Dauphin Island. Pensacola now had between ten and fourteen thousand men ready to fight. The moment everyone had waited for and refused to think about but prepared for was finally coming.[284] Everything in Mobile was supposed to be ready for a siege.

Chapter 9

MARCH 1865

Stubbornness and Spanish Fort

Ye hills repeat, ye winds the anthem bear,
Ye mountains echo back the deep refrain.
But list; another sound, low, sweet, but clear,
Harmonious blending with the louder strain—
A nation kneels, praying with low, hushed breath,
"Give Liberty" O'God, "give Liberty or Death!"[285]

The Third Presbyterian Church on Jackson Street held services every night, inviting all soldiers to attend.[286] Now $100 in gold equaled $5,000 in Confederate money, well beyond what most could pay.[287] A Ladies Fair was held at the Odd Fellows Hall to raise funds for the Twenty-fourth Alabama Infantry.[288] Basic foodstuffs continued to come into the city, as D.L. Campbell advertised a fine lot of peas, flour and other produce,[289] but prices were high. The very best people were beginning to suffer.[290] Richmond, Virginia, the capital of the Confederacy, would be threatened before the end of the month.[291]

Mobile citizens were restless in March, but it did not relate to the Union soldiers preparing to attack the city. The Mobile Sheriff's Office and the military were going from house to house, searching for bales of cotton and seizing what they found. There was an order from the Confederate government to seize all cotton stored in the city. They had already seen Union forces appropriate every pound of cotton in Savannah, Georgia, when it surrendered, and they did not want a repeat in Mobile; in their minds, the only option was to burn it up.²⁹² The soldiers assigned to this duty were somewhat surprised at how much cotton was found in the best mansions in the city. They sent draymen, presumably slaves, to gather up and trundle it to a location north of the city known as Orange Grove:²⁹³

> *Every house…is being rigidly searched and cotton is discovered where no one would suspect its existence—many a patriotic—war-meeting—"local Confederate" citizen has a score of cotton bales tumbled from the doors and windows of his private residence into the street. In some cases it has been found under floors or buried in cisterns—I heard of one who had a single bale disguised as a bed—covered with sheets and blankets with an innocent pillow at the head.*²⁹⁴

The military was quick to judge those who had kept cotton in their private residences, but those who chose to remain in Mobile and could not fight understood this differently. They had to secure income for their families when the Yankees came. Storing cotton was a matter of prudent and natural forethought, not treason. Taking steps to secure the well-being of families should not have been viewed as a crime. They were not like the speculators who were hoarding large quantities of cotton but rather honest people who hoped to trade it for Yankee money.²⁹⁵

Movements of Union forces toward Mobile were expected any day, but nothing had been reported.²⁹⁶ The weather, the endless rain and cold, slowed the Union operations.²⁹⁷ The Confederate government never gave up on trying to recruiting more men to fight, but by March there would be a dramatic turn. Instead of voicing concern for all the states in the Confederacy, the territory to defend was now only Mississippi and Alabama. If Mobile were taken in the Federal assault, then both of those states would fall quickly under Union control.

Federal movements on March 2 increased the anticipation of a future attack. Lieutenant Colonel Williams, who eagerly awaited the coming Union forces, told his wife of his excitement when the enemy forces were reported in the neighborhood of Point Clear, Alabama.²⁹⁸

At the Mobile Theatre, plays were still a daily occurrence; productions such as *The Jewess* and *Jenny Lind Come at Last* still filled the house.²⁹⁹ It would be two more days before the city would be informed of the upcoming attack, and the news was not good. The intended attack on Mobile appeared to be a heavy one, with troops and materials collecting at Dauphin Island, Fort Morgan and Fort Gaines. Everyone knew that Union forces would come, but they were not sure where they would initially begin the assault. If there was to be a direct invasion of Mobile, then all noncombatants were encouraged, yet again, to leave.[300]

Major General Dabney Maury resumed his efforts to get those who would or could not fight to leave the city. He made it clear that the moment that Union troops set foot on Mobile soil, everything that rested between the cannon fire would be destroyed—houses, fences, trees and any other objects that interfered with the range and effect of their guns would be destroyed or removed. "During an attack upon the city, all persons within its limits will be greatly exposed to the enemy's fire and extreme distress may be occasioned among non-combatants in a protracted siege."[301]

Not only did General Maury have to contend with those stubborn people who would not leave the city again, but the Confederate Exchange Commission was also still working to get captured Confederate soldiers returned home. While the practice of exchanging prisoners was not an unwelcome event, it still brought with it additional challenges in which he did not have the time to invest. Numbering 175 men,[302] these prisoners were from nearby Ship Island, New Orleans and the Battle of Mobile Bay.[303] Unfortunately, these exchanged prisoners brought with them smallpox, a loathsome disease that had been kept under control by sanitary and precautionary regulations in the city: "The former exchange of prisoners in our Bay brought some subjects who had it, and communicated the disease; and we learn that the exchanged prisoners expected tomorrow have enough of the disease already, we trust it will soon end. Oh, could we return the Yellow Jack."[304]

The steamboats such as the *Clipper*, *Johnson* and *Gertrude* from Pickensville, Alabama, still ran up the Mobile River, and there was a train that could easily carry passengers out of the city. A few Mobilians left the city, but many remained. Not only did they remain in the city, but they also did nothing toward self-preservation. They did not put back any sort of provisions or make plans to retire to the country to escape the oncoming battle. Many who stayed were still certain that the city would not fall.[305]

The misguided hope of victory could be the reason why they continued selling slaves and catching escaped slaves in the city. During most of March, an advertisement in the *Mobile Advertiser and Register* announced an upcoming estate sale that had horses, cows and slaves. There were three young men for sale: Tim, sixteen years old; Jim, fourteen years old; and John, fourteen years old.[306] The final public sale of slaves in Mobile, possibly that of the entire state of Alabama and among the last of the Confederacy, happened

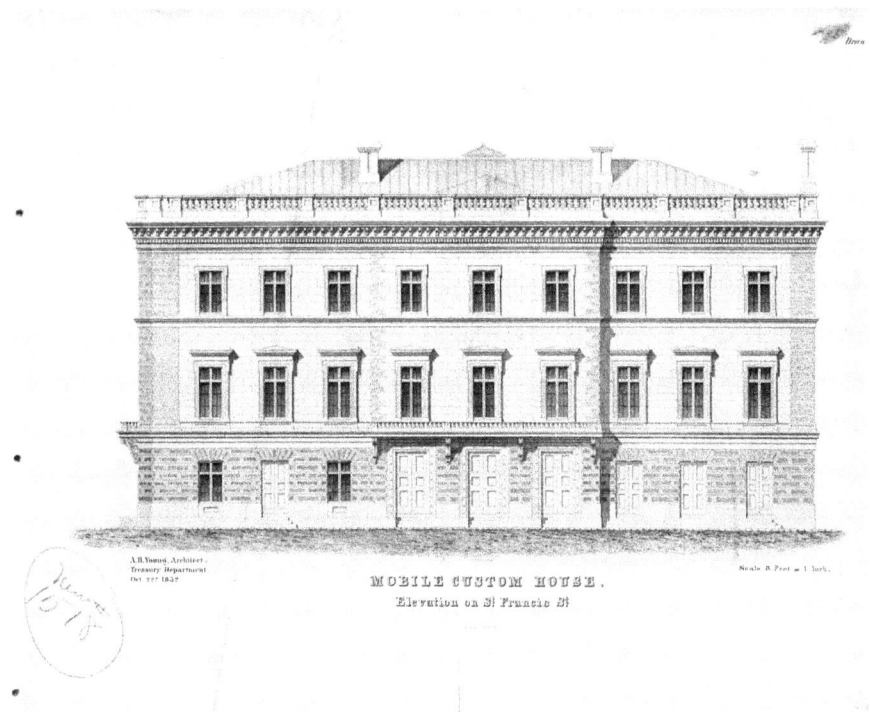

Customhouse in Mobile, Alabama, where the last documented slave auction in Mobile was held. "U.S. Custom House & Post Office, Royal & Saint Francis Streets, Mobile, Alabama." *Courtesy of the Library of Congress.*

on March 17, 1865. It was held by the firm Brooks & Ketchum at 1:30 p.m. on Royal Street in front of the Customhouse. These three remaining slaves were sold with a lot of fine mules, a fine mare and colt.[307] There was also a dramatic increase in slaves attempting to escape from their masters since Union forces were so close: "The Register…reported that the number of runaways was increasing and that five such cases had been handled in the last Mayor's Court. The penalty for a slave who was found guilty in Mayor's Court of harboring a runaway was fifty lashes unless his case was referred to the City Court, the next highest tribunal in Mobile."[308]

On March 12, 1865, Mobile began receiving reports from signal officers; seven Yankee gunboats were anchored in front of the Dog River bar, and six others sailing up to join them. They also reported as many as twenty-one thousand Union troops at Mobile Point and Dauphin Island.[309] The upper fleet was reported to be increasing, and it was clear that an attack on Mobile was coming: "So far as our information extends there are twenty-one vessels on Dog River bar; twelve of them gunboats, the balance tin-clad and tenders. They may open fire at any time, either to feel our batteries or attempt their capture.—The hostile fleet fired several shots at the Eastern and Western shore. Some of the shells fell at the Magnolia Race Course, and one of them played sad havoc with a stable."[310]

The Union forces slowly began working their way up toward Mobile by land, out of Pensacola, and by sea. Twenty-odd monitors, gunboats and transports could be seen at the water line of defenses, hugging the Eastern Shore, opposite of the city of Mobile. They were still unsure of exactly where the enemy would attack:[311]

> *On Saturday morning the fact soon passed from mouth to ear that a large flotilla was steaming up the bay, and everybody thought the hour of struggle at hand. We confess to the feelings of intense gratification at pride which we experienced at the effect of this stern fact upon the public. It produced nothing like an alarm less a panic. Every woman, so far from packing up to run, mounted their horses and got into carriages to ride down the bay "to the front," to see what was going on. There they scanned with the naked eye, and through lorgnettes, and spy-glasses the long line of Yankee monsters, some at anchor on the Eastern Shore and some still steaming up from the lower bay. Two monitors steered up the western bank, where General Cockrell opened on them with a battery, to which the iron-clad monitors, secure in their armor, replied at a distance of a mile and a quarter. The rascals fired well, and one of their shells burst not far behind the General and his staff, and created a stampede in a carriage load of ladies whose curiosity was speedily satisfied at that particular point. The shot smashed a few fence panels and tore a big hole in a gentlemen's garden, but nobody was hurt. The monitors, satisfied with their performance, then steamed over to their consorts on the opposite shore.*[312]

Everyone in Mobile was waiting for a direct attack, but the ships that were part of the attack could no longer be seen from shore. If they meant to attack Mobile, then why were they waiting? The *Mobile Advertiser and Register* made a few suggestions. First, if they tried a direct attack on the city, they could not take it. Second, they could capture Mobile easier by cutting off communications and waiting for it to fall. In either case, the people of Mobile would remain cool and defend the last great sea coast of the Confederacy.[313]

The attempts to remain calm and collected in the city were good, but there was still an air of panic. It also seems that while there was a push to shut down the drinking saloons and parlors in the previous few months, it did not stop all the soldiers from getting drunk and dangerous. A Confederate soldier, W.L. Waites of the Douglas' Texas battery, was caught drunk and punished. He came to the Office of the Commandant of the Post with a knife: "Isaac Hart, the office Sergeant, while attempting to get out of his way was overhauled by Waites and fatally stabbed. Hart lingered until about 1 o'clock yesterday and died. Waites, immediately upon inflicting the blow, attempted to make his escape brandishing the knife. The sentinel on duty was ordered to fire. He obeyed his orders and the ball took effect in the head of Waites, causing instant death."[314]

In an effort to build Confederate forces, the Negro Enlistment Bill was finally carried by one majority in the Confederate Senate in Richmond, Virginia, long after many people in the South had changed their minds regarding slaves fighting on behalf of the Confederacy. It appeared that it was only passed because General Robert E. Lee, commander of the Confederate forces, simply told them that if the Confederate army did not use the black soldier, the Union would. The Confederate army began to enroll black soldiers into its forces, no longer allowing Yankees the monopoly.[315]

Just outside Mobile's coastline, Union blockaders continued to sit at anchor six miles below the water obstructions, but this time, behind them, there were many more ships sitting in wait: "In the lowest bay, there are still some thirty odd craft of all descriptions moving about with a good deal of activity, and consuming a vast amount of Lincoln's greenbacks in coal. We report all quiet, with the presence of a hostile army and fleet in our front."[316]

On March 17, the day everyone had waited for, the moment that the entire city of Mobile had waited on for months, finally arrived. Union general Canby began his military move against Mobile.[317] On March 18, Confederate pickets recoiled before the Federal advance up the western shore of Mobile Bay.[318]

The question "if creoles, free blacks and slaves" should fight for the Confederacy quickly changed to "when should creoles, free blacks and slaves" begin to fight. There were still many creoles and free men of color in the city, and now there was a call for Confederate officers to begin to fight: "Now is a good opportunity to test the question if slaves will make good soldiers in defense of their homes. Call upon the citizens to enroll all slaves between the ages of eighteen and forty-five, to be organized for defense alone; and order all who are not so enrolled and organized within one week, to leave the city."[319]

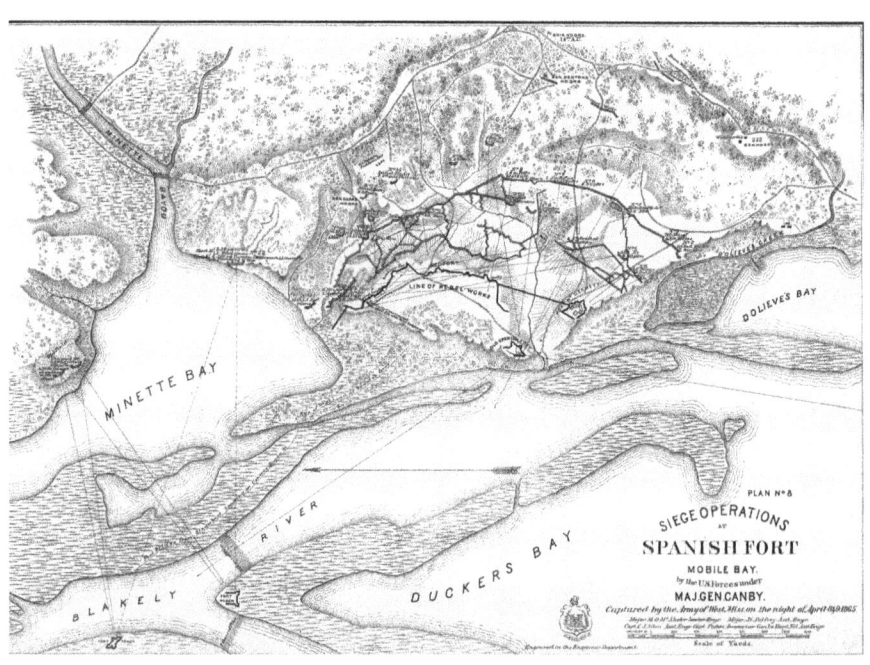

Left: Union general Edward Sprigg Canby. *Courtesy of the Library of Congress.*

Below: Siege of Spanish Fort, Mobile Bay. *Courtesy of the Library of Congress.*

The city of Mobile or the batteries on the Eastern Shore were going to be attacked at any moment, and yet those in the city still struggled to keep things as normal as possible. The Mobile & Ohio Railroad resumed after previous shutdowns, bringing large amounts of supplies to the city markets, but the prices were still too high for many to afford. The Mobile Theatre also continued to have productions almost every evening. "The Theatre still continues as our only place of amusement. The management will spare no exertions to render the performances attractive and interesting."[320]

On March 21, citizens were told of a column of Union forces advancing from Cedar Point to a place known as the Narrows, south of Mobile.[321] Every man in Mobile capable of bearing arms was told to immediately attach himself to some company for local defense.[322] The roar of Union cannon fire could be heard all through the city.[323]

As the days progressed, the city would receive various forms of news. Federal forces were reported at Fish River, just south of the city, with eighteen transports. Four Confederate regiments were sent to the Narrows to meet the Union forces, but heavy rain resulted in swollen creeks and stopped the advancement. Sixteen Union vessels could now be seen in front of the city:[324] "The Union forces did not march directly against the city but against Spanish Fort on the Eastern Shore of the Bay. Spanish Fort, an old structure which had been erected when the Spaniards held West Florida, was located twelve miles below Mobile on a tongue of land jutting into the Bay."[325]

After word of Union movements, events in the surrounding area began to develop quickly. Every boat in Mobile was pressed, and the night before the battle was spent transporting whatever was necessary for the siege.[326] On March 27, the Battle of Spanish Fort began on the Eastern Shore, across from the city.[327] Mary Waring wrote in her journal, "Today the enemy commenced operations by an attack in Spanish Fort, where some of our best troops under Gen. Gibson, were stationed. The firing was heavy and continuous, while the booming of heavy Artillery was heard distinctly on this side, rendering us very uneasy as to the fate of our brave and gallant boys stationed in and around the fort. Being unaccustomed to such heavy firing, we were, of course, much startled and excited until we gradually became used to the sound."[328]

Many people in Mobile waited, prayed and watched as the battle commenced. Sara D. Eggleston recalled:

> *As I heard the guns before Richmond in the early stage of the war, I could now, in the last stage, hear those at Spanish Fort across the Bay from Mobile for the attack on that place had begun. I was attending the service at Trinity Church,*

the distant booming of the cannon being heard from time to time above the voice of the minister and the responses of the congregation, when I heard the sound of shuffling fleet along the aisle, and looked towards the door. I saw some men in threadbare gray bearing a coffin towards the chancel. Without a word being exchanged between strangers and the minister the service of the unknown dead commenced, all the congregation devoutly taking part. Who was he? Only an obscure soldier who the day before, had been brought over from Spanish Fort mortally wounded and had died that morning in a hospital.[329]

The *Mobile Advertiser and Register* stressed that every man in Mobile, young and old, should have his arms and ammunitions pouch in readiness for emergencies. There was a haze in the atmosphere, making it difficult to see the status of the battle by glass or signal.[330] The fight commenced, and the rattle of small arms could be heard distinctly with the roar of heavy guns.[331] "From morning to night the roar of big guns vibrated in every part of the city, and with good eyes, peering through the haze of the atmosphere, the white puffs of bursting shells were discernable."[332]

Hospital boats and other service vessels traveled between Mobile and the Eastern Shore, bringing word of the status of the fight. There was some shelling of the Mobile side of the bay, by gunboats around the Race Course at the end of Shell Road, but those gunboats later steered toward the Eastern Shore:[333] "The anxiety to hear from the front of battle on the Eastern Shore of the Bay, is of course very great, as the boats arrive every hour or two, there is a crowd of people, men and women on the wharf to learn the news and make eager inquires about friends. But there is nothing like panic, as there is no reason to believe otherwise than this attack upon Mobile with a view to the capture will fail."[334]

The moment everyone in the city had waited for over the last seven months had now happened. There was a deep and severe battle between Union and Confederate forces just across the Mobile Bay. Mary Waring, from one of the families who chose to not abandon the city, ended the month with reporting that she could hear the firing still going on at the Eastern Shore. The Battle for Spanish Fort raged for days, and the Confederate troops were still fighting. Mary continued her day and her life as she had in the past. There were a few changes: her music teacher's son had just left to fight at Spanish Fort, and she spent her afternoon picking lint for the poor wounded soldiers and took a walk down Government Street[335] to find a clear view of the battle. But Mary's world, and those of her status in Mobile society, was changing. The conclusion of the Civil War was only a matter of weeks away, and the world that everyone knew in Mobile at this time would dramatically change beyond what any of them could have ever known.

Chapter 10

APRIL 1865

The Bitter End

> *'Twas on the twelfth of April*
> *Just before the break of day*
> *A message went from Anderson*
> *To Beauregard to say*
> *If you don't give up that fort*
> *You may call me a liar*
> *If I don't give the orders*
> *For the boys to open fire.*[336]

The month of April saw a quick and tragic end to many things for those loyal to both the Confederacy and the Union. Confederate president Jefferson Davis abandoned Richmond.[337] The capital of the Confederate States of America was occupied by Union troops.[338] Confederate general Robert E. Lee surrendered to Union general Ulysses S. Grant.[339] Finally, the most tragic of events: President Abraham Lincoln was murdered by J. Wilkes Booth at Ford's Theatre, Washington, D.C.[340]

The Battle of Spanish Fort continued as the Battle of Blakeley began on April 2, 1865. William Rix recalled:

> *The siege lasted some ten days, and, as night fell on the last day, there arose such a startling outburst of great guns—mortars tossing into the air fiery shells—the fleet, held at bay two or three miles below, pitching solid shots into the water batteries that lined the Spanish river in front and beyond the*

Battle of Blakeley. *Courtesy of the Delaney Collection, History Museum of Mobile, compiled by Nick Beeson.*

fort—each and every appliance of war put to work at once—brought every citizen out, and every window and balcony that looked out upon the scene was filled with heads that thought doomsday had come.[341]

The surrender of Spanish Fort would happen on April 8, and the Battle of Blakeley, the last major battle of the Civil War, took place on April 9, 1865. Matthew Woodruff wrote in his journal after the battle, "The 21st Missouri Veteran Volunteer Infantry Regiment and other units, outnumbering the Southern forces better than four to one, overpowered the two forts on April 8th and 9th, 1865—and General Robert E. Lee at the same time surrendered at Appomattox Court House in Virginia. The terrible War Between the States was over."[342]

A letter from William F. Fulton to his sister summed up the feelings of many who remained in Mobile: "Dear Sister, I have a sad tale to tell you. Mobile has fallen and we are now under Yankey domination."[343] As a fourteen-year-old living off Royal Street in downtown Mobile, William and other Confederate sympathizers could not hold back their disappointment on April 10 when they learned of the surrender. He traveled up and down the docks asking for help but was not able to get transportation out of the city. William's mother, Mrs. D.H. Fulton, was in despair when she wrote, "Willie tried all he could to find some way for us to get off but has not succeeded yet…I set up until two or three o'clock trying to hide away anything I could from the Yankees if I could not get off."[344]

On April 11, Mary D. Waring commented, "This day has passed away without my accomplishing a thing except watching our soldiers as they passed by and now and then seeing a friend and saying Adieu." She witnessed the First Louisiana Regiment, established in the city for the past eight months, pass by her place on the way to the steamboats headed up the Alabama River. She then visited a friend, Mollie, and took a short walk down Government Street, "finding everyone looking very sad and melancholy."[345]

William Fulton later slipped out of his home and down to the wharf that dreary morning. Standing on the dockside, quietly watching and experiencing that strange mix of fear and excitement, he witnessed "the last of the Confederate Army leave the city before daybreak."[346] The Confederate garrisons of Battery Huger and Battery Tracy, located at the water's edge, escaped with the rest. He saw the steamboats leave, full of gray coats and their guns, with single stacks puffing dark air in the wind. The blockade runners followed, dual stacks pushing out dark smoke and filling the air with a sooty smell to add to the gunpowder scent still noticeable in the salty air from the Battle of Blakely. Finally, he saw the gunboats, which brought up the rear. R.P. Strong, signal officer of the U.S. Army, observed the very same Confederate ships pass by his post at 6:15 a.m.: "No steamers observed at the wharves at Mobile. Three river steamers and apparently two blockade runners have just passed up Alabama River and disappeared."[347]

There are accounts of the unrest in Mobile between the time the Confederates left and the time the Union troops entered the city:

> *The morning of surrender—The streets were filled that morning as in the season of Mardi Gras. And the tide in the different thoroughfares set in one direction, converging toward the government warehouses on Water*

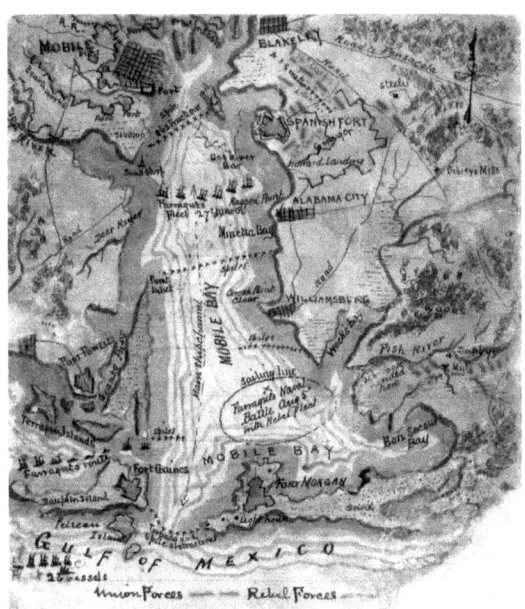

The capture of Mobile Bay.
Courtesy of the Library of Congress.

Dr. George Augustus Ketchum. *Courtesy of the Minnie Mitchell Archives, Oakleigh House, Mobile, compiled by Robert Peck.*

Street. The storehouses were broken open one after another and their contents seized and conveyed to the several parts of the town....All day long, like a colony of ants, men, women and children were rushing through the streets in jealous fear of not getting their share—some with drays and carts, but most with nothing but their hands.[348]

On April 12, at about eleven o'clock, many of those who stayed, unless they were locked in their homes with their shuttered windows closed, saw the solemn figures of Mayor R.H. Slough, Caleb Price and Dr. George Ketchum as they traveled by carriage (with a sheet performing the duty as a white flag of surrender) down Bay Shell Road toward the meeting place at Catfish Point. Dr. Ketchum would be one of the few who would see firsthand the beginning of the

Confederate States of America and its dramatic conclusion.

They were traveling to meet the Union troops landing at the lower tollgate on the bay road to negotiate the terms of surrender. Union major general Gordon Granger demanded the immediate and unconditional surrender of the city. He informed Mayor Slough, since the military presence had left, that the city was menaced by a large land and naval force. They demanded an immediate and unconditional surrender.[349] Lieutenant Colonel R.G Laughlin, of the Ninety-fourth Illinois Volunteers, and Lieutenant Commander S.R. Franklin, U.S. Navy, staff of Admiral Thatcher, presented the request to Mayor R.H. Slough the morning of April 12, and he was quick to agree to their formal request for surrender.

Union major general Gordon Granger. *Courtesy of the Library of Congress.*

As Mayor Slough, Price and Dr. Ketchum rode the five miles to Catfish Point in their carriages, there was quite a bit of action taking place on the water, just off the Mobile coastline. According to E.R. Hutchens:

> *Here we saw the grandest sight during our entire enlistment. Our corps, the Thirteenth, on transports, with the entire navy, started slowly across to the city, whose complete outline was visible. The gunboats, provided with machines for raising torpedoes, went in advance. From every transport and gunboat floated numerous flags; the soldiers and sailors in blue completely covered the boats, while the gunboats, cleared for action, kept up a continuous signaling. Add to this, the curving outline of the shore fringed with forest trees peculiar to that sunny clime, and you have a picture of marvelous beauty. As we were nearing the shore, Admiral Thatcher, commanding the*

fleet, ran his flagship alongside of General Granger's headquarters-boat, and with great dignity said to Granger, "I propose to shell the shore." To this the general replied, "You'll shell a flag of truce, if you do," and so he would, for on looking closely an old negro was seen on shore waving a white handkerchief.[350]

While General Granger met the city's mayor, Robert H. Slough, and his team trotting down the Bay Road toward them in a carriage bearing a white flag, an account from an Iowa soldier noted that they immediately began to land in Mobile, with water shallow enough that they could get off the boats and walk to land. When they reached the sandy shores, the Union troops celebrated.[351]

William saw Union troops as he walked out on the gallery at his residence: "I saw some soldiers dressed in blue going along Royal Street. I called Ma & she said that they were Yankees who had come to hoist the flag of the Dis-United States over Mobile." The soldiers went into the Battle House, ate dinner and then went on top of the building and hoisted the "gridiron" flag on the flagstaff. "As soon as they hoisted it, they took off their caps & gave three cheers for the capture of Mobile."[352]

Unexpected events were happening in Mobile while the United States flag flapped in the wind above the Battle House. When the first blue uniforms appeared in the city, instead of loud explosions of shelling or the steady eruption of torpedoes being triggered just off the coast, the residents of Mobile knew what had happened. Later, when the Yankee soldiers marched into Mobile, most citizens remained indoors, but some welcomed the conquerors. "The Yankees are being received with loud hurrah by assembled traitors," Mrs. Pillians observed.[353] Unionist and Confederate sympathizers alike headed to Royal Street, where events were unfolding, and lingered around the Customhouse, eager to know what would happen to their city.

William, with his excellent and very detailed account of that day, continued, "Mayor Slough returned with a Yankey Officer in the carriage." It is believed this officer was none other than General Granger. The mayor made an effort to be hospitable to the extent that he escorted the general to the Manassas Club room at the Battle House for a cigar.

They then walked across the street, an eager crowd following, to the front of the Customhouse, and Mayor Slough made a short speech to the crowd that had gathered around. The flag of the United States replaced the Confederate flag flying over the Customhouse soon after the speech. This party of gentlemen, in a situation committed as formally and honorably as possible, then rode the carriage back toward the Bay Road to meet the second carriage with other Union officers.

Confirmation of the surrender was spreading quickly throughout the city. Union officers began to replace all the Confederate flags in Mobile with those of the United States. Places where the flag was replaced included the market, churches all over the city and Springhill College. Later on that afternoon, a Union boat arrived at the wharf at the foot of Government Street. Union sympathizers and newly freed blacks saw the boat and rushed down the street shouting and hurrahing. They shook hands with the Yankees and were invited by them to go on the boat, and soon the deck was crowded.[354] "The negroes were very glad to meet them. They shook hands with the Yanks telling them that they were glad they had come, for they (the negroes) had been 'waiting a long time for them to come.'"[355]

When General Canby and other officers were searching for places in town to set up their headquarters, a number of prominent homes were chosen, and the current residents were told to leave. Mrs. Margaret Irwin, still a British subject, displayed a British flag on her front gallery at Oakleigh Place, declaring it neutral ground. It worked in keeping Union officers from using her home as living quarters.[356] In some cases, a situation was worked out where Union officers would stay at the homes if they were allowed rooms and if the ladies and available servants would attend to them. In one case, General Canby sent two officers to stay at one home full of ladies who had been asked to leave earlier, but he canceled the order. The ladies had begged him not to send them, but he replied, "Oh, yes, then you won't be troubled any more. Said he would send two gentlemen for protection. So we will be obliged to take them."[357]

Union general Edward Canby chose for himself the Ketchum Home on Government Street. Mrs. Ketchum's husband, Major William H. Ketchum, was still away with his troops, and Mrs. Ketchum was still there with her family and servants. The now former slave who remained at the home took things into her own hands by inviting the general to tea and suggesting that Mrs. Ketchum propose to the general that he remain at her house as a guest:[358]

> *The lady begged and pled and finally General Canby decided that only he and his orderly would occupy the Ketchum home, while his main headquarters would be located across the street and requested Mrs. Ketchum to remain as his housekeeper. Of course, there was joyful assent to this and for the remainder of his stay in Mobile, the General resided in the Ketchum home. When the Major returned after having been paroled, he approached*

William H. Ketchum House, 400 Government Street, Mobile, Alabama. *Courtesy of the Library of Congress.*

his home, but was stopped outside by a sentry who refused him permission to enter. "But it is my home!" he cried. The sentry however was adamant and only when he had gotten a pass from the proper authority could he enter his own home. The General greeted the returned soldier warmly. And when the next meal time came around, General Canby vacated his place at the head of the table in favor of the master of the house, seating himself at the side of the table. And in this friendly style, he remained a guest in the Ketchum home for the remainder of the Federal occupation of Mobile.[359]

The one home in town that was not taken for quarters in the city was that of Octavia LeVert. Those still struggling with Union soldiers in Mobile did not like how welcoming she was to those who had just taken the city. She saw Union soldiers in the city as a sign that the war was over and it was finally time for peace between the North and the South. "She threw her house open to the Yankees and went to all entertainments given by them. Her flippant explanation of conduct was, 'I've always liked the military!'"[360]

Those in the city who still had the ability to purchase the basics, maybe put a few staples back in case of emergency or had their means supplemented

Madame Octavia LeVert's House, 151 and 153 Government Street, Mobile, Alabama. *Courtesy of the Library of Congress.*

from military support were capable of surviving. The wives, mothers and children of those Confederate soldiers who had not returned were still in great need, and earlier actions like the bread riots would not feed their families. Union soldiers who traveled through the city reported on how the people looked sad and sorry, the shelves in the stores empty but for flies and the dust. "Soldiers of the Union army, who were expected to burn and destroy, have been seen to empty their haversacks, distributing their coffee and bread to staving women and children."[361]

As if defeat were not hard enough to bear, President Abraham Lincoln was assassinated at Ford's Theatre in Washington, D.C., on April 14, 1865. Mobile was already going through an immense amount of unrest, so when the news of President Lincoln's assassination came to the city, it was yet another frightening experience for those who were already in the throes of change. The city, well known for rumors, was fearful that the Union soldiers and local black residents would rise and murder the citizens. This was far from the truth, but everyone united, went to General Canby and asked him to go to Reverend Mr. Thomas W. Conway, general superintendent of freedmen, and to have him prevent an insurrection by the freedmen.[362]

Assassination of President Abraham Lincoln. *Courtesy of the Library of Congress.*

In an effort to solidify the fact that no one in Mobile had any involvement with the death of Lincoln, they gathered at the Odd Fellows Hall. Judge Chamberlain presided over this well-attended meeting. "Judge Chamberlain stated that people of Mobile condemned the act as both unmanly and diabolitical—condemned alike by the good people of the North and the South, as by those of the civilized world."[363]

In the span of one month, April 1865, the people of Mobile experienced a change in country, three changes in presidents and a complete change to the way they had lived for the entirety of their lives. Slavery was now illegal, and any money they had invested in the practice was lost. The Confederate dollar became worthless overnight. The lives of those who had struggled to stay home in Mobile to escape the war had the conflict and all its tragedy come to them. Things would never be the same.

Chapter 11

AFTER THE WAR

Union Occupation

> *A people's voice! We are noble yet,*
> *Tho' all men else their nobler dreams forget,*
> *We have a voice with which to pay the debt,*
> *Of boundless love, reverence, and regret.*[364]

When Mobile surrendered and Union forces entered the city, the change in the life of those who had lived here was dramatic. It was not the end of a lifestyle, with all its terrible parts, that this community had adopted just before the Civil War but rather the conclusion of an existence that was practiced for generations before the war. The city had recognized slavery since its existence, prior even to Alabama becoming a state within the United States, and this change would take time to become accepted. Kate Hopkins wrote her husband, who had left the city days before it was surrendered, "Oh, I have missed you so much & would give worlds to see you & yet I would not have you here. It is enough for me, a woman, to live in a captured city but I could not stand it patiently to see my husband live where he could not express his sympathies for our noble cause."[365]

Octavia LeVert and those associated with her did not feel this way. She continued to entertain the Union officers in her home and ignored the growing complaints of those around her. Kate Hopkins also shared her feelings about Mrs. LeVert with her husband: "Mrs. LeVert has a house full of Yankee officers all the time—gave them a reception & a dinner party. At the dinner was Genl Canby, Genl Granger, Genl, Commodore Palmer and another gentleman—genl I should say. Miss McKinstry was also there. It is said Mr. L & Miss McK. are both spies & have been for the Federals for some time....LeVert drove by here three times on horseback with a Yankee officer....We don't speak to or visit them."[366]

The hate and animosity toward Octavia LeVert would only increase in the coming months. She was accused of being traitor and a spy, was spit at when driving around town and was physically threatened.[367] Toward the end of the summer of 1865, most likely in fear for her personal safety and that of her daughters, she packed up what she could and left the city. She never returned to Mobile. "There is rumor in Mobile that Madame LeVert, like George Washington Cable, in neighboring New Orleans, was told to leave the city 'between suns,' but nothing is found to uphold this rumor except the fact that she did slip away from Mobile."[368]

Octavia LaVert was financially able to leave, but there were many who were not. Edward Bloch's family continued to remain in the city and survive. Since Confederate money was no longer worth the paper it was printed on, the only way to purchase anything in the city was with United States money, also known as greenbacks. During these early days, they were very scarce and could hardly be had for love or money.[369]

Edward Bloch's family just happened to have a twenty-dollar note. His mother kept the money safe just in case:

> *At the time when Mobile was captured and all our Confederate money became worthless, the only thing we had to start with was one twenty dollar bill, U.S. currency, known in these days as greenbacks, which came into our possession as a souvenir of the battle of Shiloh, where a United States paymaster's train was captured and a friend of the family, Leopold Straus, gathered up a number of bills which he sent to my Aunt Goldstucker with the request that he distribute them among the family as souvenirs of the battle. The soldiers had been in the high glee at capturing the money, some of them has lit cigars with the bills. When my Mother called on my aunt with my brother Godfrey and myself and was shown the letter and the bills, the twenty dollar note attracted my attention and my Aunt gave it to me. I had expected to keep it to play with, but my careful mother took possession of it and preserved it—she was apparently the only one to whom it has ever occurred that we might some time again use Yankee money. It would have been considered unpatriotic of anyone to have saved U.S. currency in those days.*[370]

Working with the torpedoes. *Courtesy of the Delaney Collection, History Museum of Mobile, compiled by Nick Beeson.*

Edward used this money to help support his family during the Union occupation of the city.

One objective of the Union army was to reopen the Mobile port. It would be months before a trip to Mobile would be anything but a perilous passage, as boats watched for torpedoes that still lined the channel.[371] If the port was functioning, then they could ship out the cotton they had captured and bring an economic base back to the city. This could not happen until they removed the torpedoes that still floated just under the waters of Mobile Bay. In May 1865, they had blown up thirty Union navy vessels.[372]

Another goal of the Union forces in town was to move into place the newly formed Freedmen's Bureau, created to help former slaves transition to freedom. Congress had established the Bureau of Refugees, Freedmen and Abandoned Lands on March 3, 1865.[373] Mr. Thomas W. Conway, general superintendent of the freedmen, was placed over those former slaves in and around Mobile: "All persons formerly held as slaves, will be treated in every respect as entitled to the rights of freedmen, and such as desire their services, will be required to pay for them. Care will be taken not to disturb abruptly the connections now existing, and all colored persons having places or employment, are advised to remain; whenever, the persons by whom they are employed recognize their rights and agree to compensate them for their services."[374]

The sudden changes in April 1865 slowly melted into everyday life, with everyone adjusting the best they could. The loyal Confederates protested in small ways, such as walking in the street rather than under the United States flag that flew over the sidewalk in front of the Ketchum Home,[375] where Union general Canby resided. Augusta Evans, who continued writing well past the end of the war, refused the courting of any Northern officers.[376] She finally married Confederate colonel Lorenzo Madison Wilson in 1868, and their home, Ashland, became the literary center of Mobile.[377] When Laura Roberts Pillians's husband returned from Mississippi, she, like many others in Mobile, had to make a decision: "So almost like magic every army this side of the Mississippi has melted away and left us no defense against the despotism that will rule us. I turn the first leaf in the life of humiliation I must hearafter lead."[378]

The final blow to the city, the event that would set back all efforts of growth in the near future, happened on May 25, 1865. Union forces brought all the surrendered Confederate ammunition downriver to be stored in a three-story cotton warehouse one street back of the Mobile River. It is presumed that the last of the shells were going in when one of them accidentally ignited. None of the survivors lived to tell the story. Twenty brick blocks were blown up, and between four hundred and five hundred persons were killed.[379]

While the city was surrendered to Union forces only a little more than a month before to save it from destruction, the ammunition explosion would damage the city instead:

> *So terrible was this explosion, that eight blocks were blown down, and every house in the city more or less injured....Two thirds of the buildings blown down were on fire, while every two or three minutes shells were exploding sending their fragments in all directions added to the flames of the demolished buildings, many steamers lying at the levee, and from 8000 to 10,000 bales of cotton were also burning, which rendered the scene still more grand and awful. Thousands of men worked hour after hour among the debris and brought forth one after another of the writhing and dead victims. Some had legs blown off; some an arm; some with heads crushed, and some in such condition as to present anything but the semblance of a human being. The scene agonizing beyond expression.*[380]

It was as if this final tragic event removed the last bit of strength the city had to fight. In Mobile and for its citizens, the war was done. In the upcoming years, there would still be struggles—Union against Confederate, black

Explosion of the U.S. Magazine in Mobile. *Courtesy of the Delaney Collection, History Museum of Mobile, compiled by Nick Beeson.*

against white—but nothing that would divide the country so dramatically as the Civil War. The war experience was an exhausting and dramatic one for each who played his or her part. After the surrender, the soldiers who fought for the Confederacy signed the necessary papers to join the United States of America once again, but they did not welcome Union control with open arms. In Mobile's unique world, they had experienced war, peace, freedom, surrender, humiliation, financial ruin and a host of other issues within those challenging eight months.

Let this small story of a deeply Southern city conclude with Major General Dabney H. Maury's speech to his men at the Cuba Station surrender: "Conscious that we have played our part like men, confident of the righteousness of our cause, without regret for our action in the past, and without despair of the future, let us tomorrow with the dignity of veterans who are the last to surrender perform the duty which has been assigned to us."[381]

Notes

Foreword

1. DeLeon, *Four Years in Rebel Capitals*, 56.
2. *Debow's Review* 28, no. 3, "Mobile—Its Past and Present," 309; Rix, *Incidents of Life in a Southern City*.
3. Russell, *My Diary North and South*, 137.
4. Smith and Smith, *Mobile*, iv.
5. For the best overall summaries of antebellum Mobile, see Amos, *Cotton City*, 1–47.
6. *Debow's Review* 28, no. 3, "Mobile—Its Past and Present," 310–12. General information compiled from City of Mobile Directories, 1859, 1860, 1861, Mobile Public Library, Local History and Genealogical Division, Mobile, Alabama.
7. Bergeron, *Confederate Defense of Mobile*, 13–15.
8. Andrews, *History of the Campaign of Mobile*.
9. *Debow's Review* 28, no. 3, "Mobile—Its Past and Present," 313.

Chapter 1

10. Brewer, *Alabama, Her History, Resources, War Record, and Public Men*.
11. Ibid.
12. Bloch, "Edward Bloch's Memoirs."

13. Hamilton, *Mobile of the Five Flags*.
14. Delaney, *Remember Mobile*.
15. Newspaper article from Minnie Mitchell Collection, History of Confederate States of America, 1861–65 folder.
16. Andrews, *History of the Campaign of Mobile*.
17. Ibid.
18. DeLeon, *Four Years in Rebel Capitals*.
19. Tucker, Pierpaoli and White, *Civil War Naval Encyclopedia*.
20. Massey, *Refugee Life in the Confederacy*.
21. Reid, "Negro in Alabama," 265
22. Frear, "Augusta Jane Evans Wilson."
23. Delaney, *Remember Mobile*.
24. Evans and Sexton, *Southern Woman of Letters*.
25. Ibid.
26. *Macon (GA) Daily Telegraph*, "Banks at Mobile."
27. Reid, *After the War*.
28. Ross, *Cities and Camps of the Confederate States*.
29. Mosby, "When Farragut Passed the Forts."
30. *Charleston (SC) Mercury*, "News from Mobile."
31. Massey, *Refugee Life in the Confederacy*.
32. Maury, *Recollections of a Virginian*.
33. Mosby, "When Farragut Passed the Forts."
34. DeBeauchamp, "Home of Controversial Lady Demolished."
35. Massey, *Refugee Life in the Confederacy*.
36. *(VA) Southern Illustrated News*, "News."

Chapter 2

37. Duganne, "Poetry," *New Orleans Times*.
38. *Mobile Evening Telegraph*, "Notice," August 6, 1864.
39. Goodrow, *Mobile during the Civil War*.
40. "Non-Combatants," 1864, article from Mobile, Alabama newspaper.
41. *Charleston (SC) Mercury*, "Telegraphic. Three Tening Movements at Mobile."
42. Mosby, "When Farragut Passed the Forts."
43. Ibid.
44. Ibid.
45. Rix, *Incidents of Life in a Southern City*.
46. *(LA) Daily Picayune*, "Mobile Naval Engagement."

47. *Mobile Evening Telegraph*, "From Below," August 6, 1864.
48. Ibid.
49. Rix, *Incidents of Life in a Southern City*.
50. Ibid.
51. *Daily Richmond (VA) Examiner*, "War News."
52. *(LA) Daily True Delta*, "Story of a Mobile Refugee."
53. Mobile City Council, "Mayor Appeals for Defense of City."
54. *Macon (GA) Daily Telegraph*, "Mobile."
55. Ibid., "Latest from Mobile."
56. *(LA) Daily True Delta*, "Story of a Mobile Refugee."
57. *Daily Columbus (GA) Enquirer*, "Mobile, Alabama."
58. *Macon (GA) Daily Telegraph*, "Latest from Mobile."
59. *Daily Columbus (GA) Enquirer*, "Telegraphic."
60. *Daily Richmond (VA) Examiner*, "Situation at Mobile," August 20, 1864.
61. *Macon (GA) Daily Telegraph*, "Non-Combatants."
62. Goodrow, *Mobile during the Civil War*.
63. *Macon (GA) Daily Telegraph*, "Fort Powell—the Navy."
64. *Daily Richmond (VA) Examiner*, "Situation at Mobile," August 20, 1864.
65. *Macon (GA) Daily Telegraph*, "From Mobile."
66. Ibid.
67. *Macon (GA) Daily Telegraph*, "Betting Drinks."
68. *Daily Richmond (VA) Examiner*, "Situation at Mobile," August 24, 1864.
69. *Mobile Evening Telegraph*, "From Below," August 24, 1864.
70. *Daily (LA) Picayune*, "Admiral Farragut's Own Report Official."
71. *Mobile Evening Telegraph*, "Mr. Editor." August 24, 1864.
72. *Macon (GA) Daily Telegraph*, "Mobile."
73. *Mobile Advertiser and Register*, "Committed."
74. Mosby, "When Farragut Passed the Forts."

Chapter 3

75. Creight, "Mobile," *Mobile Daily Tribune*, September 25, 1864.
76. Boyer, *Enduring Vision*.
77. DeBow, "Times in the Confederacy."
78. *Macon (GA) Daily Telegraph*, "Treasure Found."
79. Jewett and Allen, *Slavery in the South*.
80. *Mobile Advertiser and Register*, "Local Intelligence," September 1, 1864.
81. Ibid.

82. Williams and Folmar, *From that Terrible Field*.
83. Ibid.
84. *Macon Daily Telegraph*, "From Mobile," September 20, 1864.
85. *Mobile Advertiser and Register*, "Local Intelligence," September 2, 1864.
86. Ibid., "Local Intelligence," September 4, 1864.
87. Ibid., "Select Female Institute," September 10, 1864.
88. Ibid., "Local Intelligence," September 4, 1864.
89. Ibid., "The Fashions."
90. Evans and Sexton, *Southern Woman of Letters*.
91. Delaney and LeVert. "Excerpts of 'Madame Le Vert's Diary.'"
92. Williams and Folmar, *From that Terrible Field*.
93. Sellers, *Slavery in Alabama*.
94. Mobley, "Siege of Mobile," 250–70.
95. Jewett and Allen, *Slavery in the South*.
96. Sellers, *Slavery in Alabama*.
97. "Celie's Story," e-mail message.
98. *Mobile Daily Tribune*, "$250 Reward."
99. Storey, *Loyalty and Loss*.
100. *Mobile Advertiser and Register*, "Story of a Mobile Refugee."
101. Maury, *Recollections of a Virginian*.
102. Ibid.
103. *Mobile Advertiser and Register*, "Distinguished Personages."
104. Ibid., "City Affairs of the Week."
105. Ibid., "From Below," September 20, 1864.
106. Williams and Folmar, *From that Terrible Field*.
107. Parrish, *Richard Taylor*.
108. *Mobile Daily Tribune*, "Fuke…," September 25, 1864.
109. Ibid., "City Affairs," September 25, 1864.
110. *Mobile Advertiser and Register*, "To the Editors of the Advertiser and Register."

Chapter 4

111. McPhail, "Father Abram J. Ryan."
112. *New York Herald*, "Affairs in Mobile Bay."
113. Hannings, *Every Day of the Civil War*.
114. Williams and Folmar, *From that Terrible Field*.
115. *Mobile Advertiser and Register*, "Criminal Law."
116. *New York Herald*, "Affairs in Mobile Bay."

117. *Mobile in Photo-Gravure.*
118. *Mobile Advertiser and Register*, "Drowned."
119. Jewett and Allen, *Slavery in the South.*
120. *Mobile Advertiser and Register*, "Mobile and Ohio Railroad."
121. Ibid., "Local Intelligence," October 6, 1864.
122. Pickenpaugh, *Captives in Blue.*
123. *Daily True Delta and Confederate*, "Mobile," October 6, 1864.
124. *(LA) Daily Picayune.* "Mentions."
125. *Daily True Delta and Confederate*, "Mobile," October 6, 1864.
126. Fornell, "Mobile During the Blockade."
127. Rix, *Incidents of Life in a Southern City.*
128. Ibid.
129. *Mobile Advertiser and Register*, "Local Intelligence," October 9, 1864.
130. Ibid., "From Below," October 11, 1864.
131. Ibid., "Farragut."
132. *Daily True Delta and Confederate*, "Mobile," October 15, 1864.
133. Owen, *Our Women in the War.*
134. *Mobile Advertiser and Register*, "City Bar-Rooms," October 18, 1864.
135. Brooks, "War Memoirs."
136. Ibid.
137. Bergeron, *Confederate Defense of Mobile.*
138. Ibid.
139. Ibid.
140. Ibid.
141. Williams and Folmar, *From that Terrible Field.*
142. Ibid.
143. *Mobile Advertiser and Register*, "Enrollment of Men of Color."
144. Slap, Towers and Goldfield, *Confederate Cities.*
145. Bailey, *Neither Carpetbaggers nor Scalawags.*
146. Levine, *Confederate Emancipation.*

Chapter 5

147. *Mobile Advertiser and Register*, "I'm Conscripted, Smith, Conscripted," November 23, 1864.
148. *Mobile Advertiser and Register*, "City Affairs for the Week," November 6, 1864.
149. Ibid., "Cold Weather," November 23, 1864.
150. Wikipedia, "United States Presidential Election, 1864."
151. Noe, *Yellowhammer War.*

152. *Mobile Advertiser and Register*, "From Below."
153. Cappon, *History of Alabama during the Civil War*.
154. Wikipedia, "Peter U. Murphey."
155. *Mobile Advertiser and Register*, "Personal," November 6, 1864.
156. Land, *Mobile, Her Trade, Commerce and Industries*.
157. *Mobile Advertiser and Register*, "City Affairs for the Week," November 20, 1864.
158. Ibid., "Theatre," November 5, 1864.
159. Ibid., "Theatre," November 23, 1864.
160. Bloch, "Edward Bloch's Memoirs."
161. Ibid.
162. Ibid.
163. Ferris and Greenberg, *Jewish Roots in Southern Soil*.
164. Moses, *History of the Jews*.
165. Bloch, "Edward Bloch's Memoirs."
166. Ibid.
167. *Mobile Advertiser and Register*, "Ball Last Night."
168. Ibid., "City Affairs for the Week," November 20, 1864.
169. Ibid., "Local Intelligence," November 4, 1864.
170. Ibid., "Garden Seeds," November 2, 1864.
171. *"Our Women in the War,"* 1885.
172. *Mobile Advertiser and Register*, "Mayor's Court."
173. Rix, *Incidents of Life in a Southern City*.
174. *Mobile Advertiser and Register*, "Inquests."
175. Ibid., "Present Crisis—No. V."
176. Levine, *Confederate Emancipation*.
177. Coopersmith, *Fighting Words*.

Chapter 6

178. *Mobile Advertiser and Register*, "Christmas 1864."
179. Huffstodt, "Last Great Assault Campaigning for Mobile."
180. *Mobile Advertiser and Register*, "City Affairs for the Week," December 4, 1864.
181. Ibid., "The River."
182. Ibid., "City Affairs for the Week," December 4, 1864.
183. Ibid., "The City," December 25, 1864.
184. Ibid., "New Steamer."
185. Ragan, *Confederate Saboteurs*.
186. Mobley, "Siege of Mobile," 250–70.

187. *Mobile Advertiser and Register*, "Municipal Elections," December 5, 1864.
188. Ibid., "Municipal Elections," December 4, 1864.
189. Ibid., "Elections Yesterday."
190. Ibid., "New Boards."
191. Ibid., "Theatre," December 11, 1864.
192. Ibid., "The City."
193. Ibid., "Handsome Demonstration."
194. Semmes, *Memoirs of Service Afloat*.
195. Delaney, "Raphael Semmes."
196. Ibid.
197. Semmes, *Memoirs of Service Afloat*.
198. Ibid.
199. *Mobile Advertiser and Register*, "Compliment to Commander Semmes."
200. Ibid., "Flag of Truce Boat."
201. Ibid., "Relief of Prisoners."
202. Scott, Lazelle, Davis et al., *War of the Rebellion*.
203. *Mobile Advertiser and Register*, "Supper Tonight."
204. Williams and Folmar, *From that Terrible Field*.
205. *Mobile Advertiser and Register*, "Situation About Mobile."
206. Mobley, "Siege of Mobile," 250–70.
207. *Mobile Advertiser and Register*, "Wood."
208. Cumming and Barksdale, *Kate*.
209. *Mobile Advertiser and Register*, "Situation Below Mobile."
210. Ibid., "From Below."
211. Cumming and Barksdale, *Kate*.

Chapter 7

212. Evans, "God Bless the South and Bring Us Peace."
213. DeBow, "Times in the Confederacy."
214. *Mobile Advertiser and Register*, "Catawba Wine."
215. Ibid., "Metals Wanted."
216. Ibid., "News for the Week."
217. Cappon, *History of Alabama during the Civil War*.
218. *Mobile Advertiser and Register*, "New Year."
219. Diary of Laura Roberts Pillians.
220. *Mobile Advertiser and Register*, "Battery Tracy."
221. Mobley, "Siege of Mobile," 250–70.

222. Evans and Sexton, *Southern Woman of Letters*.
223. Lisarelli, *Last Prison*.
224. *Mobile Advertiser and Register*, "Fort Gaines Prisoners."
225. Ibid., "Exchange of Prisoners."
226. Ibid., "Fort Gaines Prisoners."
227. Williams and Folmar, *From that Terrible Field*.
228. Ibid.
229. Rix, *Incidents of Life in a Southern City*.
230. Mobley, "Siege of Mobile," 250–70.
231. *Mobile Advertiser and Register*, "Despondency."
232. DeBow, "Times in the Confederacy."
233. *Mobile Advertiser and Register*, "Drunkenness in the Army."
234. Ibid., "Hail Storm."
235. Ibid., "Market Gardeners Are in Great Despair."
236. Ibid., January 15, 1865.
237. Cumming and Barksdale, *Kate*.
238. *Mobile Advertiser and Register*, "Local Intelligence," January 15, 1865.
239. Ibid., "Prices."
240. Ibid., "Local Intelligence," January 29, 1865.
241. Mobley, "Siege of Mobile," 250–70.
242. Bridgman, *Calendar of the Civil War*.
243. *Mobile Advertiser and Register*, "Negro Question."
244. Ibid., "Burning of the Rose Maury."
245. Ibid., "Firing Yesterday."
246. Ibid., January 29, 1865.
247. Woodruff and Boney, *Union Soldier in the Land of the Vanquished*.
248. *Mobile Advertiser and Register*, "Shameful Neglect."

Chapter 8

249. *Mobile Advertiser and Register*, "Nothing to Drink."
250. Bridgman, *Calendar of the Civil War*.
251. Cumming and Barksdale, *Kate*.
252. *Mobile Advertiser and Register*, "Sheriff's Sale."
253. Ibid., "Steamboats."
254. Ibid., "Indian Pain Killer."
255. Mobley, "Siege of Mobile," 250–70.

256. *Mobile Advertiser and Register*, "Marine's List."
257. Newspaper article from Minnie Mitchell Collection, History of Confederate States of America, 1861–65 folder.
258. Cumming and Barksdale, *Kate*.
259. Moore, *Brief History of Women's Role*.
260. DeBow, "Times in the Confederacy."
261. University of South Alabama, "Temperance Hall."
262. *Mobile Advertiser and Register*, "Ball Last Night."
263. Ibid., "Creole Fair."
264. Mumfort, "From a Confederate Diary."
265. *Mobile Advertiser and Register*, "Closing of the Barrooms."
266. Ibid., "Mayor's Office."
267. Webb, *Mobile Mayor's Court Reports*.
268. *Mobile Advertiser and Register*, "Closing the Drinking Saloons."
269. Ibid., "Negro Soldiers."
270. Ibid., "Mobile."
271. Ibid., "Fact in Aid of Theory."
272. Ibid., "Woman's Thoughts."
273. Ibid., "Society of Loyal Confederates."
274. Reid, "Negro in Alabama," 265
275. Ibid.
276. Cumming and Barksdale, *Kate*.
277. Goodrow, *Mobile during the Civil War*.
278. Scott, Robert N., Lazelle, Davis et al., *War of the Rebellion*.
279. Maury, *Recollections of a Virginian*.
280. Ibid.
281. Williams and Folmar, *From that Terrible Field*.
282. *Mobile Advertiser and Register*, "Mobile."
283. Diary of Laura Roberts Pillians.
284. *Mobile Advertiser and Register*, "Enemy Movements," February 28, 1865.

Chapter 9

285. Adele, "To the South Wind," *Mobile Advertiser and Register*.
286. *Mobile Advertiser and Register*, "Local Intelligence," March 1, 1865.
287. DeBow, "Times in the Confederacy."
288. *Mobile Advertiser and Register*, "Twenty-forth Alabama."
289. Ibid., March 17, 1865.

290. Newspaper article from Minnie Mitchell Collection, History of Confederate States of America, 1861–65 folder.
291. Bridgman, *Calendar of the Civil War*.
292. *Mobile Advertiser and Register*, "Military Orders."
293. Rix, *Incidents of Life in a Southern City*.
294. Williams and Folmar, *From that Terrible Field*.
295. *Mobile Advertiser and Register*, "Cotton."
296. Ibid., "Enemy Movements," March 1, 1865.
297. Williams and Folmar, *From that Terrible Field*.
298. Schell, *Fort Powell and the Civil War*.
299. *Mobile Advertiser and Register*, "Mobile Theatre."
300. Ibid., "Enemy Movements," March 4, 1865.
301. Maury, "Headquarters, District of the Gulf."
302. *Mobile Advertiser and Register*, "Arrival of Prisoners."
303. Ibid., "Return of Prisoners."
304. Ibid., "Small Pox."
305. Ibid., "Doom of Mobile."
306. Ibid., "Horses, Cows and Negroes for Sale," March 9, 1865.
307. Ibid., "Horses, Cows and Negroes for Sale," March 17, 1865.
308. Mobley, "Siege of Mobile," 250–70.
309. *Mobile Advertiser and Register*, "Enemy Movements." March 12, 1865.
310. Ibid., "City Affairs for the Week."
311. Ibid., "Enemy Movements." March 14, 1865.
312. Ibid., March 14, 1865.
313. Ibid.
314. Ibid., "Fatal Affair."
315. Ibid., "Mobile."
316. Ibid., "Mobile Bay."
317. Bridgman, *Calendar of the Civil War*.
318. Huffstodt, "Last Great Assault Campaigning for Mobile."
319. *Mobile Advertiser and Register*, "Defense of the City."
320. Ibid., "Affairs in the City for the Week."
321. Ibid., "From Below."
322. Ibid., "Military."
323. Ibid., "Local Intelligence," March 21, 1865.
324. Ibid., "The Enemy," March 22, 1865.
325. Goodrow, *Mobile during the Civil War*.
326. Rix, *Incidents of Life in a Southern City*.
327. Bridgman, *Calendar of the Civil War*.

328. Harrison and Holt, *Miss Waring's Journal*.
329. *"Our Women in the War,"* 1885.
330. *Mobile Advertiser and Register*, "The Enemy," March 28, 1865.
331. Ibid., "The Front."
332. Ibid., "War About Home."
333. Ibid., "The Enemy," March 30, 1865.
334. Ibid., "The News."
335. Harrison and Holt, *Miss Waring's Journal*.

Chapter 10

336. Bloch, "Edward Bloch's Memoirs."
337. Stewart, *Jefferson Davis's Flight from Richmond*.
338. Montgomery, *Leading Facts of American History*.
339. Ibid.
340. Bridgman, *Calendar of the Civil War*.
341. Rix, *Incidents of Life in a Southern City*.
342. Woodruff and Boney, *Union Soldier in the Land of the Vanquished*.
343. "Dear Sister," William Fulton to Mrs. J.A. Pettus.
344. "My Own Darling Child," Mrs. D.H. Fulton to Mrs. J.A. Pettus.
345. Harrison and Holt, *Miss Waring's Journal*.
346. "Dear Sister," William Fulton to Mrs. J.A. Pettus.
347. Scott, Robert N., Lazelle, Davis et al., *War of the Rebellion*.
348. Rix, *Incidents of Life in a Southern City*.
349. Scott, Robert N., Lazelle, Davis et al., *War of the Rebellion*.
350. Hutchins, *War of the 'Sixties*.
351. Trudeau, *Out of the Storm*.
352. "Dear Sister," William Fulton to Mrs. J.A. Pettus.
353. Doyle, *New Men, New Cities, New South*.
354. "Dear Sister," William Fulton to Mrs. J.A. Pettus.
355. Ibid.
356. United States Department of Interior, National Register of Historic Places, "Oakleigh."
357. Hopkins, "My Beloved Husband."
358. Goodrow, *Mobile during the Civil War*.
359. Glennon and Glennon, *Alabama History on the Air!*
360. Satterfield, *Madame Le Vert*.
361. *Cincinnati*, "From Mobile."

362. Ibid.
363. Ibid.

Chapter 11

364. Evans and Sexton, *Southern Woman of Letters*.
365. Hopkins, "My Beloved Husband."
366. Ibid.
367. Satterfield, *Madame Le Vert*.
368. Ibid.
369. Hopkins, "My Beloved Husband."
370. Bloch, "Edward Bloch's Memoirs."
371. Reid, *After the War*.
372. Hopkins, "My Beloved Husband."
373. Reid, "Negro in Alabama," 265.
374. *Cincinnati*, "From Mobile."
375. Goodrow, *Mobile during the Civil War*.
376. Fitzgerald, *Urban Emancipation*.
377. Fremault, "Made Best-Sellers of Her Novels."
378. Diary of Laura Roberts Pillians.
379. Goodrow, *Mobile during the Civil War*.
380. "Yankee Captain's Reports on Mobile Like Travel Ad."
381. "Head Quarters, Maury's Division," Dabney H. Maury to Soldiers.

BIBLIOGRAPHY

BOOKS

Amos, Harriet E. *Cotton City: Urban Development in Antebellum Mobile.* Tuscaloosa: University of Alabama Press, 1985.

Andrews, C.C. *History of the Campaign of Mobile: Including the Cooperative Operations of Gen. Wilson's Cavalry in Alabama.* New York: D. Van Nostrand, 1867.

Bailey, Richard. *Neither Carpetbaggers nor Scalawags: Black Officeholders during the Reconstruction of Alabama, 1867–1878.* Montgomery, AL: R. Bailey Publishers, 1991.

Bergeron, William Arthur, Jr. *Confederate Defense of Mobile 1861–1865.* Baton Rouge: Louisiana State University, 1980.

Boyer, Paul S. *The Enduring Vision: A History of the American People.* Boston: Houghton Mifflin, 2007.

Brewer, Willis. *Alabama, Her History, Resources, War Record, and Public Men: From 1540 to 1872.* Montgomery, AL: Barrett & Brown, Steam Printers and Book Binders, 1872.

Bridgman, Raymond L. *Calendar of the Civil War: Including Every Military and Naval Engagement (Except the Smallest Skirmishes), the Secession Conventions, Presidential Nominations, Calls for Troops, Peace Negotiations, Important Army Movements and Other Events of Interest.* Boston: Press of Rockwell and Churchill, 1890.

Cappon, Lester Jesse. *The History of Alabama during the Civil War.* Madison: University of Wisconsin Press, 1922.

Coopersmith, Andrew Seth. *Fighting Words: An Illustrated History of Newspaper Accounts of the Civil War.* New York: New Press, 2004.

Bibliography

Cumming, Kate, and Richard Barksdale. *Kate: The Journal of a Confederate Nurse.* Baton Rouge: Louisiana State University Press, 1998.
Delaney, Caldwell. *Remember Mobile.* Mobile, AL, 1948.
DeLeon, T.C. *Four Years in Rebel Capitals.* Alexandria, VA: Time-Life Books, 1983.
Doyle, Don Harrison. *New Men, New Cities, New South: Atlanta, Nashville, Charleston, Mobile, 1860–1910.* Chapel Hill: University of North Carolina Press, 1990.
Evans, Augusta J., and Rebecca Grant Sexton. *A Southern Woman of Letters: The Correspondence of Augusta Jane Evans Wilson.* Columbia: University of South Carolina Press, 2002.
Ferris, Marcie Cohen, and Mark I. Greenberg. *Jewish Roots in Southern Soil: A New History.* Waltham, MA: Brandeis University Press, 2006.
Fitzgerald, Michael W. *Urban Emancipation: Popular Politics in Reconstruction Mobile, 1860–1890.* Baton Rouge: Louisiana State University Press, 2002.
Glennon, Robert M., and John F. Glennon. *Alabama History on the Air!: Mobile Radio Broadcasts of the 1930s.* Fairhope, AL: Robert M. Glennon, 2009.
Goodrow, Esther Marie. *Mobile during the Civil War.* Mobile, AL: Historic Mobile Preservation Society, 1950.
Hamilton, Peter J. *Mobile of the Five Flags: The Story of the River Basin and Coast about Mobile from the Earliest Times to the Present.* Mobile, AL: Gill Print, 1913.
Hannings, Bud. *Every Day of the Civil War: A Chronological Encyclopedia.* Jefferson, NC: McFarland, 2010.
Harrison, Mary Douglass Waring, and Thad Holt. *Miss Waring's Journal: 1863 and 1865, Being the Diary of Miss Mary Waring of Mobile, during the Final Days of the War Between the States.* Chicago: Wyvern Press of SFE, 1964.
Hutchins, Edward R. *The War of the 'Sixties.* New York: Neale Publishing Company, 1912.
Jewett, Clayton E., and John O. Allen. *Slavery in the South: A State-by-State History.* Westport, CT: Greenwood Press, 2004.
Land, John E. *Mobile, Her Trade, Commerce and Industries, 1883–4: Manufacturing Advantages, Business and Transportation Facilities, Together with Sketches of the Principal Business Houses and Manufacturing Concerns in the "Gulf City."* Mobile, AL: J.E. Land, 1884.
Levine, Bruce C. *Confederate Emancipation: Southern Plans to Free and Arm Slaves during the Civil War.* Oxford, UK: Oxford University Press, 2006.
Lisarelli, Danial Francis. *The Last Prison: The Untold Story of Camp Groce CSA.* Parkland, FL: Universal Publishers, 1999.
Massey, Mary Elizabeth. *Refugee Life in the Confederacy.* Baton Rouge: Louisiana State University Press, 1964.
Maury, Dabney Herndon. *Recollections of a Virginian in the Mexican, Indian, and Civil Wars.* New York: C. Scribner's Sons, 1894.

Mobile in Photo-Gravure: From Recent Negatives. Mobile, AL: E.O. Zadek Jewelry, 1892.

Montgomery, D.H. *The Leading Facts of American History*. New York: Chautauqua Press, 1891.

Moore, Albert B. *A Brief History of Women's Role in the Confederacy*. N.p., n.d. Minnie Mitchell Archives, Oakleigh.

Moses, Alfred G. *A History of the Jews of Mobile*. Baltimore, MD: Lord Baltimore Press, 1916.

Noe, Kenneth W. *The Yellowhammer War: The Civil War and Reconstruction in Alabama*. Tuscaloosa: University of Alabama Press, 2014.

"Our Women in the War": The Lives They Lived; the Deaths They Died. Charleston, SC: News and Courier Book Presses, 1885.

Owen, Thomas McAdory. *Our Women in the War: Memorial to the Women of the Confederacy*. Montgomery, AL?, 1905.

Parrish, T. Michael. *Richard Taylor: Soldier Prince of Dixie*. Chapel Hill: University of North Carolina Press, 1992.

Pickenpaugh, Roger. *Captives in Blue: The Civil War Prisons of the Confederacy*. Tuscaloosa: University of Alabama Press, 2013.

Ragan, Mark K. *Confederate Saboteurs: Building the Hunley and Other Secret Weapons of the Civil War*. College Station: Texas A&M University Press, 2015.

Reid, Whitelaw. *After the War: A Southern Tour*. Cincinnati, OH: Moore, Wilstach & Baldwin, 1866.

Rix, William. *Incidents of Life in a Southern City during the War: A Series of Sketches Written for the Rutland Herald*. N.p., 1880.

Ross, Fitzgerald. *Cities and Camps of the Confederate States*. Urbana: University of Illinois Press, 1958.

Russell, William Howard. *My Diary North and South*. Edited by Eugene H. Berwanger. Baton Rouge: Louisiana State University Press, 2001.

Satterfield, Frances Gibson. *Madame Le Vert: A Biography of Octavia Walton Le Vert*. Edisto Island, SC: Edisto Press, 1987.

Schell, Sidney Henson. *Fort Powell and the Civil War: Western Approaches to Mobile Bay, 1861–1865*. Westminster, MD: Heritage Books, 2012.

Scott, Robert N., H.M. Lazelle, George B. Davis, Leslie J. Perry et al. *The War of the Rebellion: A Compilation of the Official Records of the Union and Confederate Armies*. Washington, D.C.: Government Printing Office, 1880.

Sellers, James Benson. *Slavery in Alabama*. Tuscaloosa: University of Alabama Press, 1950.

Semmes, Raphael. *Memoirs of Service Afloat during the War Between the States*. Baltimore, MD: Kelly, Piet & 1869.

Bibliography

Slap, Andrew L., Frank Towers and David R. Goldfield. *Confederate Cities: The Urban South during the Civil War Era.* Chicago: University of Chicago Press, 2015.

Smith, Sidney Adair, and C. Carter Smith Jr. *Mobile: 1861–1865.* Chicago: Wyvern Press, 1964.

Stewart, John. *Jefferson Davis's Flight from Richmond: The Calm Morning, Lee's Telegrams, the Evacuation, the Train, the Passengers, the Trip, the Arrival in Danville and the Historians' Frauds.* Jefferson, NC: McFarland, 2015.

Storey, Margaret M. *Loyalty and Loss: Alabama's Unionists in the Civil War and Reconstruction.* Baton Rouge: Louisiana State University Press, 2004.

Trudeau, Noah Andre. *Out of the Storm: The End of the Civil War, April–June 1865.* Boston: Little, Brown, 1994.

Tucker, Spencer, Paul G. Pierpaoli and William E. White. *The Civil War Naval Encyclopedia.* Santa Barbara, CA: ABC-CLIO, 2011.

Webb, Paula L. *Mobile Mayor's Court Reports 1865.* Mobile, AL: Mobile Genealogical Society, 2016.

Williams, James M., and John Kent Folmar. *From that Terrible Field: Civil War Letters of James M. Williams, Twenty-first Alabama Infantry Volunteers.* Tuscaloosa: University of Alabama Press, 1981.

Woodruff, Mathew, and F.N. Boney. *A Union Soldier in the Land of the Vanquished: The Diary of Sergeant Mathew Woodruff, June–December, 1865.* Tuscaloosa: University of Alabama Press, 1969.

Articles

DeBow, J.D. "Times in the Confederacy." *Times in the Confederacy.* http://quod.lib.umich.edu/m/moajrnl/acg1336.2-02.006/574:2?rgn=main%3Bview.

Debow's Review 28, no. 3. "Mobile—Its Past and Present" (September 1860): 309.

Delaney, Caldwell, and Octavia Walton LeVert. "Excerpts of 'Madame Le Vert's Diary.'" *Alabama Historical Quarterly* 36 (Spring 1941): 30–54.

Fornell, Earl. "Mobile during the Blockade." *Alabama Historical Quarterly* 23, nos. 1–2 (1961): 29–44. ADAH Digital Collections.

Huffstodt, James. "The Last Great Assault Campaigning for Mobile." Ms, Civil War Essays, Doy Leale McCall Rare Book and Manuscript Library/University of South Alabama.

Mobley, Joe A. "The Siege of Mobile, April 1864–August 1865." *Alabama Historical Review* 38, no. 4 (1976): 250–70.

Reid, Robert D. "The Negro in Alabama during the Civil War." *Journal of Negro History* 35, no. 3 (1950): 265.

Bibliography

Newspaper Articles

Adele. "To the South Wind." *Mobile Advertiser and Register*, March 12, 1865.
Charleston (SC) Mercury. "News from Mobile." February 18, 1864. Civil War: Antebellum to Reconstruction, 1843–77.
———. "Telegraphic. Three Tening Movements at Mobile." August 6, 1864. NewsBank.
Creight, Annie Germelia. "Mobile." *Mobile Daily Tribune*, September 25, 1864.
Daily Columbus (GA) Enquirer. "Mobile, Alabama." August 10, 1864. NewsBank.
———. "Telegraphic." August 13, 1864. NewsBank.
Daily Richmond (VA) Examiner. "Situation at Mobile." August 20, 1864. American Civil War Newspapers, 1840–77.
———. "Situation at Mobile." August 24, 1864. American Civil War Newspapers, 1840–77.
———. "War News." August 8, 1864.
Daily True Delta and Confederate. "Mobile." October 15, 1864.
———. "Mobile." October 6, 1864.
Duganne, A.J. "Poetry." *New Orleans Times*, January 14, 1865.
Evans, Augusta. "God Bless the South and Bring Us Peace." *Mobile Advertiser and Register*, January 29, 1865.
Fremault, George. "Made Best-Sellers of Her Novels in 19th Century." *Mobile Press Register*, December 26, 1936.
(LA) Daily Picayune. "Admiral Farragut's Own Report Official." August 25, 1864. American Civil War Newspapers, 1840–77.
———. "Mentions." October 6, 1864. NewsBank.
———. "Mobile Naval Engagement." August 9, 1864. NewBank.
(LA) Daily True Delta. "Story of a Mobile Refugee." August 27, 1864. American Civil War Newspapers, 1840–77.
Macon (GA) Daily Telegraph. "Banks at Mobile." February 17, 1864. Civil War: Antebellum to Reconstruction, 1843–77.
———. "Betting Drinks." August 20, 1864. American Civil War Newspapers, 1840–77.
———. "Fort Powell—the Navy." August 15, 1864. American Civil War Newspapers, 1840–77.
———. "From Mobile." August 19, 1864. American Civil War Newspapers, 1840–77.
———. "From Mobile." August 17, 1864. American Civil War Newspapers, 1840–77.
———. "Latest from Mobile." August 9, 1864. NewsBank.
———. "Mobile." August 8, 1864. NewsBank.

Bibliography

———. "Mobile." August 30, 1864. American Civil War Newspapers, 1840–77.
———. "Non-Combatants." August 15, 1864. NewsBank.
———. "Treasure Found." September 22, 1864.
Maury, Dabney. "Headquarters, District of the Gulf." *Mobile Advertiser and Register*, March 8, 1865.
Mobile Advertiser and Register. "Affairs in the City for the Week." March 19, 1865.
———. "Arrival of Prisoners." March 7, 1865.
———. "Ball Last Night." February 1, 1865.
———. "Battery Tracy." January 5, 1865.
———. "Burning of the Rose Maury." January 24, 1865.
———. "Catawba Wine." January 6, 1865.
———. "Christmas 1864." December 25, 1864.
———. "The City." December 25, 1864.
———. "City Affairs for the Week." December 4, 1864.
———. "City Affairs for the Week." March 12, 1865.
———. "City Affairs for the Week." November 6, 1864.
———. "City Affairs for the Week." November 20, 1864.
———. "City Affairs of the Week." September 11, 1864.
———. "City Bar-Rooms." October 18, 1864.
———. "Closing of the Barrooms." February 3, 1865.
———. "Closing the Drinking Saloons." February 7, 1865.
———. "Cold Weather." November 23, 1864.
———. "Committed." August 28, 1864.
———. "Compliment to Commander Semmes." December 21, 1864.
———. "Cotton." March 2, 1865.
———. "Creole Fair." February 5, 1865.
———. "Criminal Law." October 13, 1864.
———. "Defense of the City." March 19, 1865.
———. "Despondency." January 10, 1865.
———. "Distinguished Personages." September 9, 1864.
———. "Doom of Mobile." March 7, 1865.
———. "Drowned." October 2, 1864.
———. "Drunkenness in the Army." January 8, 1865.
———. "Elections Yesterday." December 6, 1864.
———. "The Enemy." March 30, 1865.
———. "The Enemy." March 28, 1865.
———. "The Enemy." March 22, 1865.
———. "Enemy Movements." February 28, 1865.
———. "Enemy Movements." March 1, 1865.

Bibliography

———. "Enemy Movements." March 14, 1865.
———. "Enemy Movements." March 4, 1865.
———. "Enemy Movements." March 12, 1865.
———. "Enrollment of Men of Color." October 22, 1864.
———. "Evacuation of Fort Powell." September 4, 1864.
———. "The Exchange of Prisoners." January 7, 1865.
———. "Fact in Aid of Theory." February 10, 1865.
———. "Farragut." October 15, 1864.
———. "The Fashions." September 23, 1864.
———. "A Fatal Affair." March 14, 1865.
———. "The Firing Yesterday." January 31, 1865.
———. "Flag of Truce Boat." December 1, 1864.
———. "Fort Gaines Prisoners." January 8, 1865.
———. "From Below." August 6, 1864.
———. "From Below." August 24, 1864.
———. "From Below." December 29, 1864.
———. "From Below." March 21, 1865.
———. "From Below." November 8, 1864.
———. "From Below." October 10–11, 1864.
———. "From Below." September 16, 1864.
———. "From Below." September 20, 1864.
———. "The Front." March 29, 1865.
———. "Garden Seeds." November 2, 1864.
———. "Hail Storm." January 11, 1865.
———. "A Handsome Demonstration." December 4, 1864.
———. "Horses, Cows and Negroes for Sale." March 9, 1865.
———. "Horses, Cows and Negroes for Sale." March 17, 1865.
———. "I'm Conscripted, Smith, Conscripted," November 23, 1864.
———. "Indian Pain Killer." February 1, 1865.
———. "Local Intelligence." January 15, 1865.
———. "Local Intelligence." January 29, 1865.
———. "Local Intelligence." March 1, 1865.
———. "Local Intelligence." March 21, 1865.
———. "Local Intelligence." November 4, 1864.
———. "Local Intelligence." October 9, 1864.
———. "Local Intelligence." October 6, 1864.
———. "Local Intelligence." September 1, 1864.
———. "Local Intelligence." September 4, 1864.
———. "Local Intelligence." September 2, 1864.
———. "Marine's List." February 5, 1865.

BIBLIOGRAPHY

———. "The Market Gardeners Are in Great Despair." January 15, 1865.
———. "Mayor's Court." November 15, 1864.
———. "Mayor's Office." February 4, 1865.
———. "Metals Wanted." January 1, 1865.
———. "Military." March 21, 1865.
———. "Military Orders." March 1, 1865.
———. "Mobile." March 15, 1865.
———. "Mobile and Ohio Railroad." October 4, 1864.
———. "Mobile Bay." March 16, 1865.
———. "Mobile Theatre." March 4, 1865.
———. "Municipal Elections." December 5, 1864.
———. "Municipal Elections." December 4, 1864.
———. "The Negro Question." January 10, 1865.
———. "Negro Soldiers." February 5, 1865.
———. "The New Boards." December 7, 1864.
———. "The News." March 30, 1865.
———. "News for the Week." January 15, 1865.
———. "A New Steamer." December 11, 1864.
———. "New Year." January 1, 1865.
———. "Nothing to Drink." February 8, 1865.
———. "Personal." November 6, 1864.
———. "The Present Crisis—No. V." November 8, 1864.
———. "Prices." January 29, 1865.
———. "Relief of Prisoners." December 10, 1864.
———. "Return of Prisoners." March 4, 1865.
———. "Select Female Institute." September 10, 1864.
———. "Shameful Neglect." January 29, 1865.
———. "Sheriff's Sale." February 16, 1865.
———. "Situation About Mobile." December 20, 1864
———. "Situation Below Mobile." December 28, 1864.
———. "Small Pox." March 5, 1865.
———. "Society of Loyal Confederates." February 24, 1865.
———. "Steamboats." February 1, 1865.
———. "Story of a Mobile Refugee." September 16, 1864.
———. "The Supper Tonight." December 21, 1864.
———. "Theatre." December 11, 1864.
———. "Theatre." November 5, 1864.
———. "Theatre." November 23, 1864.
———. "To the Editors of the Advertiser and Register." October 1, 1864.
———. "Twenty-forth Alabama." March 15, 1865.

Bibliography

———. "The War About Home." March 29, 1865.
———. "A Woman's Thoughts." February 12, 1865.
———. "Wood." December 20, 1864.
Mobile Daily Tribune. "City Affairs." September 25, 1864.
———. "Fuke…" September 25, 1864.
———. "$250 Reward." September 25, 1864.
Mobile Evening Telegraph. "Mr. Editor." August 24, 1864.
New York Herald. "Affairs in Mobile Bay." October 3, 1864. Newsbank.
Richmond (VA) Examiner. "Situation at Mobile." August 20, 1864. American Civil War Newspapers, 1840–77.
(VA) Southern Illustrated News. "News." May 7, 1864. Civil War: Antebellum to Reconstruction, 1843–77.

Websites

Delaney, Norman C. "Raphael Semmes." Encyclopedia of Alabama, May 26, 2013. http://www.encyclopediaofalabama.org/article/h-1359.
Frear, Sara. "Augusta Jane Evans Wilson." Encyclopedia of Alabama, June 26, 2013.
McPhail, Carol. "Father Abram J. Ryan: Poet, Priest, Defender of the South (Photos)." AL.com, March 22, 2013.
Mumfort, William Taylor. "From a Confederate Diary." Oocities, October 2009. http://www.oocities.org/laheavy1/MumfordDiary.html.
United States Department of Interior, National Register of Historic Places. "Oakleigh." National Park Service, Washington, D.C., 1935. http://focus.nps.gov/pdfhost/docs/NRHP/Text/71000104.pdf.
University of South Alabama, McCall Library. "Temperance Hall." http://digital.archives.alabama.gov/cdm/ref/collection/usa01/id/310.
Wikipedia. "Peter U. Murphey." July 19, 2015. https://en.wikipedia.org/wiki/Peter_U._Murphey.
———. "United States Presidential Election, 1864." November 13, 2015. https://en.wikipedia.org/wiki/United_States_presidential_election,_1864.

Bibliography

Unpublished/Undetermined

Bloch, Edward. "Edward Bloch's Memoirs." Ms, Springhill Avenue Temple Archives, Mobile, Alabama, n.d.

Brooks, Mary E. "War Memoirs." Letter. Ms. History Museum of Mobile, Museum Department, Mobile, Alabama, n.d.

"Celie's Story." E-mail message to Lauren Van Der Bijl, October 14, 2015. Minnie Mitchell Archives, Oakleigh Place, Mobile, Alabama.

Cincinnati. "From Mobile." May 10, 1865. Minnie Mitchell Archives, Oakleigh Place, Mobile, Alabama.

DeBeauchamp, Reneau. "Home of Controversial Lady Demolished." Unknown, Civil War 1861–65. Minnie Mitchell Archives, Oakleigh Place, Mobile, Alabama.

Diary of Laura Roberts Pillians, 1865. Van Autwerp Collection, DoyLeale McCall Rare Book and Manuscript Library/University of South Alabama, Mobile, Alabama.

Fulton, Mrs. D.H. "My Own Darling Child." Letter to Mrs. J.A. Pettus, April 12, 1865. Minnie Mitchell Archives, Oakleigh Place, Mobile, Alabama.

Fulton, William. "Dear Sister." Letter to Mrs. J.A. Pettus. April 12, 1865. Minnie Mitchell Archives, Oakleigh Place, Mobile, Alabama.

"Head Quarters, Maury's Division." Dabney H. Maury to Soldiers, May 7, 1865. Minnie Mitchell Archives, Oakleigh Place, Mobile, Alabama.

Hopkins, Kate. "My Beloved Husband." Letter to Mr. Hopkins, May 25, 1865. Ms, Minnie Mitchell Archives, Oakleigh Place, Mobile, Alabama.

Kilshaw Irwin Clisby to Historic Mobile Preservation Society, October 12, 1960. Minnie Mitchell Archives, Oakleigh Place, Mobile, Alabama.

Mobile City Council. "Mayor Appeals for Defense of City." News release, Mobile, 1864.

Mosby, Fannie Jane. "When Farragut Passed the Forts." 1864. TS, Civil War 1861–65. Minnie Mitchell Archives Oakleigh, Mobile, Alabama.

Newspaper article from History of Confederate States of America, 1861–65 folder. Minnie Mitchell Collection.

"Non-Combatants." 1864. Article from Mobile, Alabama newspaper. Minnie Mitchell Archives, Mobile, Alabama.

"Yankee Captain's Reports on Mobile Like Travel Ad." TS, Vertical File Civil War. Doy Leale McCall Rare Book and Manuscript Library/University of South Alabama, Mobile, Alabama.

INDEX

A

Adams-Oris Treaty 56
Alabama 8, 9, 17, 18, 22, 24, 25, 37,
    39, 41, 42, 43, 50, 51, 52, 55,
    56, 58, 59, 60, 63, 68, 70, 71,
    76, 85, 86, 88, 89, 90, 92, 93,
    94, 102, 103, 111
  Athens 51
  Decatur 50
  Mobile 70
  Pickensville 94
  Point Clear 93
  Pollard 9, 25, 71
  Prattville 55
  River 9, 20, 29
  Selma 20
Andrews, C.C., General 20
antebellum 7, 26, 56, 80
Appalachee Batteries 71
Atlanta, Georgia 35, 40

B

Baldwin County 46
Banks, Nathanial P., General 21
Barton Academy 24, 41
Battery Huger 103
Battery Tracy 75, 103
Battle House 8, 55, 61, 71, 78, 106
Battle of Mobile Bay 20, 30, 31, 46,
    47, 65, 76, 94
Battle of Nashville 74
Battle of Spanish Fort 99, 100, 101
Bay Shell Road 32, 51, 104
Beulah 21
Bloch, Edward (Jew) 17, 60, 112
Bloch, Joseph (Jew) 59, 60
blockade runners 52, 65, 77, 83, 89,
    103
Booth, John Wilkes 101
Bragg, Braxton, General 18
bread riot 61, 109
Brooks & Ketchum 95
Buckner, Simon Bolivar, General 25

C

Canby, Edward R.S., General 65, 87,
    97, 107, 108, 109, 111, 114
Catfish Point 63, 104, 105
coffee 80, 83, 84, 85, 109
Columbia, South Carolina 22
Confederate 17, 18, 20, 21, 25, 26, 31,
    33, 34, 35, 36, 37, 38, 39, 40,

Index

41, 43, 47, 51, 52, 55, 56, 57, 58, 60, 61, 63, 66, 67, 68, 70, 71, 72, 76, 77, 78, 79, 81, 82, 83, 85, 87, 88, 89, 90, 92, 93, 94, 97, 99, 100, 101, 102, 103, 105, 106, 107, 109, 110, 112, 114
batteries 37, 53
blockade runners 65
Conscription Act of 1862 46
Department of the Gulf 56
Exchange Bureau 76
Exchange Commission 94
governor of Alabama 58
gunboats 30, 37, 47
House of Representatives 81
Impressment Act of 1863 44
ironclads 50
ladies 29
mayor of Mobile 61
officers 31
secretary of war 25, 33
Senate 97
ships 103
War Department 41
conscription 46, 52, 55, 63, 77, 85
Constitutional Convention 17
Conway, Thomas W., Reverend 109
Creole Fair 85
Creoles 21, 55, 56, 85, 97
Creole Scouts 37
CSS *Alabama* 68, 70
CSS *Morgan* 31, 33, 68
CSS *Selma* 47, 58, 68
CSS *Tennessee* 31
Cummings, Kate 72, 73, 76, 79, 89
Customhouse 78, 95

D

Davis, Jefferson 57, 64, 101
District of the Gulf 25
Dog River bar 37, 39, 41, 52, 57, 74, 95, 96

E

Eastern Shore 46, 53, 71, 81, 96, 99, 100
Eggleston, Sara D. 61, 99
emancipation 81, 86
Evans, Augusta J. 21
Evans, Matt 21

F

Farragut, David Glasgow, Admiral 25, 27, 30, 31, 33, 37, 38, 53
First Louisiana Band 70
Fish River 37, 99
Ford, John Salmon, Colonel 70
foreigners 52
Forrest, Nathan Bedford, General 46, 47, 51
Forsyth, John 36, 76, 87
Forts 24
  Blakeley 47, 81
  Gaines 18, 24, 30, 31, 35, 36, 37, 38, 40, 74, 76, 93
  Morgan 8, 18, 24, 30, 33, 34, 35, 37, 38, 39, 40, 50, 77, 93
  Powell 23, 24, 25, 27, 29, 33, 34, 36, 37, 40, 41, 47, 76
  Spanish Fort 47, 99, 100, 102
  Sumter 91
free blacks 21, 44, 97
Freedmen's Bureau 113
Fulton, Mrs. D.H. 102
Fulton, William F. 102, 103, 106

G

Galvanized Yankees 90
Gardner, Frank, General 47
Goldstucker, Hannah 59
Granger, Gordon, General 105, 106, 111
Grant's Pass 23, 25, 34
Grant, Ulysses S., General 65, 101
greenbacks 97, 112
Guard House 31

Index

H

Harrison, George W., Captain 68
Havana, Cuba 20, 70, 84
Heustis, J.F. 42
Heustis, Rachel Lyons 23, 42
Holt, Mrs. Robert 84
Hood, John Bell, General 50, 58, 74, 79
Hopkins, Kate 111
Hunley 66
Hutchens, E.R. 105

I

Inez 21
ironclad 31, 33, 37
Irwin, Margaret 29, 107
Irwin, Mary K. 45
Irwin, T.K. 45

J

Jewish population 17, 59, 60
Johnson, Andrew 57
Judson Female Institute 41

K

Ketchum, George, Dr. 104
Ketchum, William H., Major 107

L

Lee, Robert E., General 97, 101, 102
LeVert, Dr. Henry 26, 43
LeVert, Octavia Walton 26, 43, 108, 111, 112
Lincoln, Abraham 57, 83, 101, 109
Louisiana Purchase 56
Lyon, James T. 62

M

Macaria 22, 23
Macon Daily Telegraph 23, 34
Magnolia Cemetery 82
Mardi Gras 68, 85, 103
Maury, Dabney, General 23, 25, 26, 30, 33, 36, 41, 46, 47, 51, 56, 58, 66, 90, 94, 115
Mayor's Court 61, 95
McKay, William G. 66
military trial 34
Minervy (Evans house servant) 21
Mississippi 39, 61, 114
Mississippi River 70
Mobile 17, 18, 20, 21, 22, 23, 25, 39, 43, 53, 54, 55
 Alabama 23, 25
 Bay 20, 23, 24, 25, 31, 32, 34, 37, 41, 44, 46, 47, 49, 51, 53, 57, 66, 74, 81, 83, 97, 100, 113
 Courthouse 83
 Creoles 56, 85
 Creole Scouts 37
 defenses 26, 76
 dock 36
 evacuees 26
 mayor of Mobile 61
 Mobile Advertiser and Register 37, 40, 41, 46, 51, 53, 64, 67, 71, 76, 78, 81, 82, 84, 87, 94, 96, 100
 Mobile County Jail 39
 Mobile Evening Telegraph 29, 31, 38
 Mobile & Great Northern 71
 Mobile Home Guard 60
 Mobile & Ohio Railroad 51, 99
 Mobile Point 95
 Mobile Theatre 39, 58, 67, 88, 93, 99
 Mobile Theatre Orchestra 59
 port 20, 113
 River 20, 30, 34, 37, 83, 94, 114
 Sheriff's Office 92
Montgomery, Alabama 17, 23, 26, 39, 59, 65
Mosby, Frances Jane 24, 30, 31, 39
Mumford, William Taylor 85
Murphy, Pat, Captain 31, 68

INDEX

N

National Day of Prayer 57
Negro Enlistment Bill 97
New Orleans, Louisiana 9, 20, 21, 30, 46, 54, 59, 71, 77, 94, 112

O

Oakleigh 29, 44, 107
Odd Fellows Hall 61, 71, 92, 110
111th Colored Troops 51
106th Colored Troops 51
110th Colored Troops 51
Orphan Brigade 55

P

Parks, Lyons and Keyland 66
Pascagoula, Mississippi 21
patterollers 40, 44
Pillians, Laura Roberts 90
Pope Leo XVIII 59
Price, Caleb 104
prisoners 25, 32, 37, 58, 71, 76, 77, 94
provost marshal 23

R

Rix, William 52, 63, 77, 101
Rose Maury 66, 81
Royal Street 26, 31, 60, 61, 78, 95, 102, 106

S

sale of slaves 94
saloons 54, 85, 86, 97
secession 17, 43
Seddon, J.A. 33
Semmes, Raphael, Admiral 68, 70, 85
Sherman, William T., General 8, 74, 87
Ship Island 71, 94
siege 26, 35, 47, 56, 61, 64, 67, 90, 91, 94, 99, 101
Sisters of Charity 55

slaves 21, 29, 44, 46, 49, 50, 51, 56, 60, 63, 64, 80, 81, 83, 86, 88, 90, 93, 94, 95, 97, 107, 110, 111, 113
  armed 64
  enlistment 64, 88
  escaped 94
  hired 44, 60
  impressed 51
  market 60
  patrol 44
  runaways 39, 40, 49, 63
Slough, Robert H. 34, 47, 54, 61, 67, 85, 104, 105, 106
Society of Loyal Confederates 88
Soldiers' Friend Society 71
spies 90, 112
Springhill College 60, 107
St. Paul, Henry, Major 66

T

Taylor, Nellie 41
Taylor, Richard, General 41, 47, 55
Temperance Hall 85
Three Mile Creek 40

U

Union 8, 17, 20, 23, 24, 27, 32, 39, 40, 43, 47, 50, 52, 56, 61, 63, 65, 66, 70, 71, 74, 77, 81, 83, 86, 90, 93, 99, 105, 106, 108, 111
  army 20, 109, 113
  blockade 41, 74, 76, 83, 97
  fleet 36
  gunboats 34, 51
  ironside 39
  navy 23, 113
  prison 58, 71
  prisoners 76
  ships 37, 41, 68
  vessels 52
Unionists 43, 46, 52, 60, 63, 77, 106
USS *Brooklyn* 36
USS *Chickasaw* 34

INDEX

USS *Hartford* 33, 36
USS *Tecumseh* 31

V

Virginia 17, 92, 102
  Fredericksburg 25
  Hampton 83
  Richmond 25, 97

W

Waring, Mary 99, 100, 102
water batteries 35, 101
Watts, Thomas H. 47, 54, 58, 87
Williams, James M., Colonel 29, 34,
    36, 37, 41, 43, 47, 55, 71, 76, 93

Y

Yankees 25, 28, 37, 38, 39
Young Men's Social Club 61

About the Author

Paula Lenor Webb is a government documents reference and outreach librarian at the University of South Alabama. She has a master's in library and information science from the University of Alabama and a BA in English from Judson College. Paula is associated with the Mobile Genealogical Society, the Mobile Historical Society and the History Museum of Mobile. Born in Mobile, the marriage of her library science degree and her love of research carried her deep into the history of her beloved home city.

Courtesy of Chase Smith.

www.ingramcontent.com/pod-product-compliance
Lightning Source LLC
Chambersburg PA
CBHW042140160426
43201CB00021B/2354